Cambridge Elements

Elements in the Global Middle Ages
edited by
Geraldine Heng
University of Texas at Austin
Susan J. Noakes
University of Minnesota–Twin Cities
Lynn Ramey
Vanderbilt University

EARLY GLOBALISM AND CHINESE LITERATURE

Yuanfei Wang
Lingnan University
Victor H. Mair
University of Pennsylvania

Shaftesbury Road, Cambridge CB2 8EA, United Kingdom

One Liberty Plaza, 20th Floor, New York, NY 10006, USA

477 Williamstown Road, Port Melbourne, VIC 3207, Australia

314–321, 3rd Floor, Plot 3, Splendor Forum, Jasola District Centre,
New Delhi – 110025, India

Cambridge University Press is part of Cambridge University Press & Assessment, a department of the University of Cambridge.

We share the University's mission to contribute to society through the pursuit of education, learning and research at the highest international levels of excellence.

www.cambridge.org
Information on this title: www.cambridge.org/9781009500159
DOI: 10.1017/9781009272360

© Yuanfei Wang and Victor H. Mair 2026

This publication is in copyright. Subject to statutory exception and to the provisions of relevant collective licensing agreements, with the exception of the Creative Commons version the link for which is provided below, no reproduction of any part may take place without the written permission of Cambridge University Press & Assessment.

An online version of this work is published at 10.1017/9781009272360 under a Creative Commons Open Access license CC-BY-NC-ND 4.0 which permits re-use, distribution and reproduction in any medium for non-commercial purposes providing appropriate credit to the original work is given. You may not distribute derivative works without permission. To view a copy of this license, visit https://creativecommons.org/licenses/by-nc-nd/4.0

When citing this work, please include a reference to the DOI 10.1017/9781009272360

First published 2026

A catalogue record for this publication is available from the British Library

ISBN 978-1-009-50015-9 Hardback
ISBN 978-1-009-27235-3 Paperback
ISSN 2632-3427 (online)
ISSN 2632-3419 (print)

Additional resources for this publication at www.cambridge.org/earlyglobalism

Cambridge University Press & Assessment has no responsibility for the persistence or accuracy of URLs for external or third-party internet websites referred to in this publication and does not guarantee that any content on such websites is, or will remain, accurate or appropriate.

For EU product safety concerns, contact us at Calle de José Abascal, 56, 1°, 28003 Madrid, Spain, or email eugpsr@cambridge.org

Early Globalism and Chinese Literature

Elements in the Global Middle Ages

DOI: 10.1017/9781009272360
First published online: February 2026

Yuanfei Wang
Lingnan University

Victor H. Mair
University of Pennsylvania

Author for correspondence: Yuanfei Wang, yuanfeiwang@ln.edu.hk

Abstract: Exploring "early globalism and Chinese literature" through the lens of "literary diffusion," this Element analyzes two primary forms. The first is Buddhist literary diffusion, whose revolutionary impact on Chinese language and literature is illustrated through scriptural translation, transformation texts, and "journey to the West" stories. The second, facilitated diffusion, engages with the maritime world, traced through the seafaring journey of Cinderella stories and the totalizing worldview in literature on Zheng He's voyages. The authors contend that early global literary diffusion left a lasting imprint on Chinese language, literature, and culture. This title is also available as Open Access on Cambridge Core.

Keywords: literary diffusion, Cinderella, Buddhism, Monkey King, Admiral Zheng He

© Yuanfei Wang and Victor H. Mair 2026

ISBNs: 9781009500159 (HB), 9781009272353 (PB), 9781009272360 (OC)
ISSNs: 2632-3427 (online), 2632-3419 (print)

Contents

	Prologue	1
	PART I BUDDHISM AND LITERATURE	6
	Introduction to Part I	6
1	Buddhist Translation and the Chinese Language	8
2	*Bianwen* ("Transformation Texts") and Their Importance	17
3	Buddhism, the Literary World, and the "Journey to the West" Stories	24
	PART II SEA AND STORY	45
	Introduction to Part II	45
4	Maritime Circulation of the Cinderella Story	48
5	Voyages of Zheng He: The World in Ming Literature	66
	Epilogue	78
	Appendix	80
	References	84

Additional resources for this publication at
www.cambridge.org/earlyglobalism

Prologue

Nearly everyone on earth knows the Cinderella story – the mistreated orphan, tormented by her stepmother, who, with a fairy's help, wins a prince's heart after he tracks her down with a glass slipper she left behind.[1] But few realize that this timeless tale, so familiar today, already existed in Greek, underwent a major transformation in India, and then journeyed to Southeast Asia, China, before circling back to Europe ages ago. Wherever the story went, it adapted, reshaping itself once again. What exactly has been enabling this quaint tale to thrive since ancient times, traversing unstoppably from one culture to another, captivating hearts worldwide? Is it because the story's unusual power of psychological suggestion has universal appeal? Or does the answer lie in the relays of the story's history of migrations?

Like the Cinderella story, the timeless stories (and the words that make them) told in this Element have been migrating across cultures for centuries, even millennia. They, too, have journeyed far and wide: from Greece and India to Southeast Asia, Inner Asia, China, Europe, and beyond. What has enabled these stories to stand the test of time and distance, securing their eternal presence in human history? Is their resilience rooted in religious faith, the pursuit of wealth through long-distance trade, the desire to tell and to hear enchanting stories, or the thirst for new knowledge? These are but a few of the possibilities. Although the focus of this Element is premodern Chinese literature and language, or literature written in Chinese characters and produced in regions that are parts of China today, we aim to contextualize premodern Chinese literature and language within premodern transregional and transcultural networks that we call "early globalism."

But what is "early globalism"? How does "globalism" differ from "globalization," a term that we encounter far more often than "globalism" nowadays? In the premodern world when a real sense of globalization had not yet occurred, smaller-scale transregional connections were already taking place and persisted. What do we call them? Geraldine Heng suggests that we refer to these smaller-scale transregional activities as "globalism," differentiating them from the more modern phenomenon of "globalization." Heng proposes that the study of globalism not only "foregrounds interconnectivity" across distances, enabling us to see "how geographical spaces and vectors were interlinked," but also "exists as a dynamic" that forms "larger scales of relation" or "forces that globalize" (Heng, 2021: 16). "Interconnectivity" includes the long-distance transport of anything such as goods, artisans, and stories over continents or

---

[1] All translations in this Element are ours unless otherwise noted. All the diacritical marks of the Sanskrit terms were purposely omitted for the convenience of the reader.

seas; "dynamics" indicate cultural, religious, or political forces such as Islam and Indic culture that transformed local populations, politics, cultures, languages, architecture, and art (Heng, 2021: 16). Further, such premodern globalism is patently uneven all over the world (Heng, 2021: 17–18).

This Element focuses on literary diffusion to discuss two types of prominent cultural activities of early globalism in premodern China, activities that evince both interconnectivity and dynamics. First is early medieval and Tang (618–907) Buddhism's influence on Chinese language and literature. The second is the growth of maritime trade and maritime interactions from the Tang dynasty onward that resulted in expansion and circulation of new knowledge. Both examples of early globalism brought forth literary diffusion.

In premodern times, stories and knowledge were circulated and disseminated in a piecemeal fashion. Stories (and in most cases, fragments of stories) were heard, retold, memorized, paraphrased, summarized, improvised, adapted, written down, commented upon, illustrated, and passed on. This dynamic process of literary diffusion proved remarkably fluid, capable of sustaining itself across centuries with no end. The routes of literary diffusion overlapped with the trade routes by land and by sea that connected civilizations. Along the routes traveled new stories, foreign words, and novel knowledge carried by merchants and monks across deserts and oceans to reach bustling oasis towns and thriving seaports in other places, and then onward to other mountains and rivers, to other shores and other lands throughout the world.

In this telling or, more precisely, retelling, of these medieval "global stories," which is itself a form of literary diffusion, particularly as related to China, both Dunhuang and the South China Sea are two crucial geographical locales that constituted the medieval global loop of trade, religions, and literatures. The desert town of Dunhuang at the far western end of Gansu Province was the jumping-off point from which the fabled Silk Road led traders and monks across the chain of oases to travel from China to Central Asia and beyond and vice versa (Hansen, 2012: 167–172) (Figure 1). It was also an essential place for Buddhist pilgrims like Xuanzang 玄奘 (602–664) to pass through on their way to India to fetch Buddhist scriptures. As such, Dunhuang became a center of Buddhist culture, even though it was in a remote location. Further, with advances in maritime technology, especially shipbuilding and the invention of the maritime compass, from the Tang dynasty onward the South China Sea became increasingly important for maritime connections between China and the world (Figure 2).

The desert and the ocean are connected and formed an early global loop. Some medieval travelers knew of this desert–sea circuit. For example, the

Early Globalism and Chinese Literature

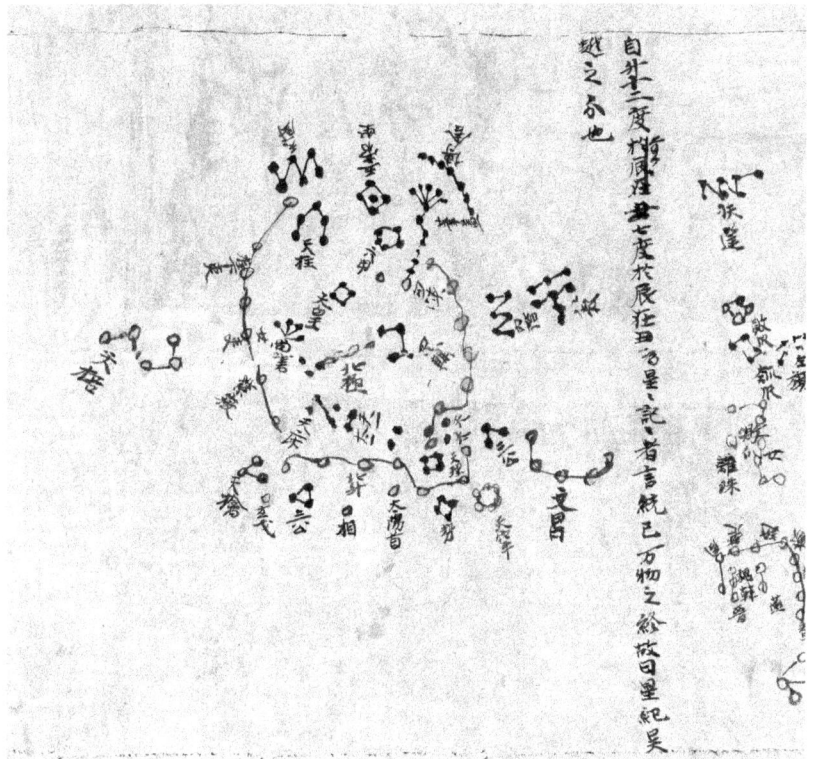

Figure 1 The thirteenth star chart of the Dunhuang Star Atlas (thirteen charts in total), the oldest complete star map in existence, dating from the second half of the seventh century CE. The chart details the part of the sky that is aligned with the North Pole. It contains 144 stars visible to the naked eye. From the British Library Dunhuang collection (Or.8210/S.3326 R.2.[8]).

Buddhist monk Faxian 法顯 (337–422) traversed overland from Chang'an through Khotan to reach India. On his trip returning to China, he took the sea route. He sailed to Sri Lanka, south of Calcutta in West Bengal, passed by Sumatra, and then headed to Shandong Peninsula (Hansen, 2012: 160–165). The desert–sea global loop will be the backdrop of China's early global stories (see Figure A1 in the Appendix and the online resources).

Before beginning to tell these stories, three concepts need to be clarified. First, the duration of China's Middle Ages is different from that of Europe. The European Middle Ages spanned from the fifth to the fifteenth century. But scholars of Chinese literature are now inclined to use "the Middle Period" to refer to the Tang (618–907), the Five Dynasties (907–797), and the Song (960–1276). They use "early medieval" to refer to the Six Dynasties

Figure 2 A traditional Chinese maritime compass (a twentieth-century duplicate, Hong Kong Maritime Museum). Photograph by Yuanfei Wang.

(220–589) up to the Tang. China's Middle Ages can be broadly defined as spanning from the Western Han dynasty (202 BCE–9 CE) to the Southern Song (1127–1279). Since there is not a single standard for "medieval/middle period" that fits both China and Europe, this Element also includes an "early modern" duration – the Ming dynasty (1368–1644) – to correspond approximately to the European Middle Ages and for the purpose of including two important examples of "literary diffusion" relating to the Ming literature on the monk Xuanzang's journey to India and Admiral Zheng He's 鄭和 (1371–1433) seven voyages (1405–1433) across the Indian Ocean.

Second, the term "Chinese literature" refers to various kinds of literature that were produced within the administrative borders of any given Chinese dynasty. In particular, this Element focuses on "Chinese popular literature and language" – works and words that belong neither to the Confucian canon nor to classical Chinese poetry. These are translated Buddhist sutras, lay Buddhist storytelling genres, tales, dramas, and novels. They contain a significant number of elements from foreign religions and cultures, exotic stories and knowledge, and colloquial expressions. There was a wide range among the members of the Chinese audience from royalty and elites, to merchants, laymen and laywomen, and, to some extent, common folk.

Third, the primary theme of this Element is literary diffusion. Whereas "globalism" signifies *any* transregional interconnectivity or dynamics, regardless of discipline or subject, "literary diffusion" concentrates on the interconnectivity and dynamics of languages and literatures across cultures. "Literary diffusion" refers to the process by which language and literature are transmitted beyond the culture in which they originated, or the process by which language and literature are created and circulated to accommodate the incoming Other. "Literary diffusion" presumes an unevenness and difference among various cultures and the existence of one or many cultural centers that generate fluxes of literary diffusion. In other words, globalism seems inevitable in a world of diversity and difference. In fact, globalism may have happened more dramatically in premodern times than we thought since the high level of unevenness of cultures in medieval times might have brought about a rapid "literary diffusion." Buddhism is a great example. In its early days, Buddhism spread very quickly from India to China and other East Asian countries where the cultures were completely different. When Buddhism reached its peak in China in the Tang dynasty and then became pervasive throughout late imperial Chinese society, this cross-cultural transmission slowed down dramatically.

Diffusion is also operative in the physical sciences. In biochemistry, channel proteins and carrier proteins assist molecules in moving across the membrane (Philibert, 1991). Likewise, in the Middle Ages, the ship was the vehicle par excellence that expedited the spread of new information to large regions of the world. Good examples of seaborne "literary diffusion" are the cases of the global spread of the Cinderella story in the Middle Ages and the voyages of Zheng He that collected a large quantity of information about Southeast Asia and the Middle East from around the Indian Ocean, along with all sorts of exotic flora and fauna, and carried them back to China.

This Element consists of two parts. Part I discusses the spread of Buddhism in China and its legacy in Chinese language and literature. Part II examines how maritime circulations facilitated literary diffusion and production in China and around the world.

PART I BUDDHISM AND LITERATURE

Introduction to Part I

Approximately 2,000 years ago, merchants from Iran, Tocharia (northern rim of the Tarim Basin), and India traversed the vast deserts between the Western Regions and China on camel and horseback to trade precious goods for their communities. Through the scorching winds, under starry skies, along trails littered with bleached bones and animal dung, these travelers whispered prayers to the Buddha for safe passage (Figure 3). Spreading their faith, they shared tales about the Enlightened One along the fabled Silk Road. But these followers of the Buddha may never have anticipated – or they may have devoutly

Figure 3 Buddha with radiate halo and mandorla. A portable shrine from the Turfan area, fifth- or sixth-century CE, in the northern branch of the Central Asian Silk Road (The Metropolitan Museum of Art, New York). Photograph by Yuanfei Wang.

believed – that centuries later, the Buddha's teachings would bear countless fruits in this foreign land.

As Arthur F. Wright insightfully notes, Buddhism's transformation of Chinese culture is "one of the great themes in the history of Eastern Asia" (Wright, 1959: 3). With the founding of Buddhism, during the Maurya empire (322–185 BCE), the teaching of the Buddha spread over the Indian subcontinent, expanding northwestward into the regions of Gandhara, Kashmir, and eastern Afghanistan. Buddhism took hold in the thriving regions of present-day Turkmenistan and Uzbekistan, and along the Amu Darya (Zurcher, 1990, 1997). Later, Iranian, Tocharian, and Indian peoples traveling along the Silk Road from northwestern India to the frontier of China's Han dynasty (206 BCE–220 CE) introduced Buddhism (see Figure A2 in the Appendix and the online resources).

The earliest Buddhist scriptures containing prescriptions to enhance intuitive faculties were well received by the Chinese, who were eager to acquire knowledge of longevity and immortality (de Bary and Bloom, 1999: 421). In one of the earliest discourses on the compatibility of Buddhism and Chinese culture, *Mouzi: Disposing of Error* 牟子理惑論, Mouzi defends Buddhism by arguing that Chinese sages like Confucius, Laozi, Yao, Shun, and the Duke of Zhou would all have applauded the foreign religion's virtues, regardless of its different cultural practices (de Bary and Bloom, 1999: 421–426). This was the very promising beginning of Buddhist teaching in China.

Part I consists of three sections. Each section focuses on one aspect of Chinese language and literature that were greatly influenced by Buddhist literary diffusion. Section 1 discusses medieval Buddhist translation as a type of literary diffusion that generated new words and discourses in China that had long-lasting impact on Chinese language and culture. Section 2 delves into how Buddhist literary diffusion gave rise to new art forms and genres. The new genre of *bianwen* that grew out of lay Buddhist oral storytelling is a case in point. The *bianwen* genre has bequeathed much to the Chinese popular literary and performance tradition. Section 3 explores how Buddhist literary diffusion created the literary world of Chinese literature. It examines popular stories of the pilgrimage to India by the legendary monk Xuanzang as influenced by the *Ramayana* and Buddhism. The most famous realization of all these stories about Xuanzang and his companions is the Ming novel *Journey to the West* (Xiyou ji 西遊記) which has been translated into English four times in the twentieth century and adapted into cartoons, animation, dramas, and films around the world. These stories are excellent examples of how the medieval literary diffusion could prompt new currents of literary diffusion that could last for hundreds of years and will possibly continue ad infinitum.

1 Buddhist Translation and the Chinese Language

The Buddhist scriptures originally were disseminated in a variety of local Prakrit vernacular languages. Later, Buddhists adopted Sanskrit, a refined literary language, to produce Buddhist literature (Nattier, 1990).[2] But the Chinese language is fundamentally different from Sanskrit and Prakrit. So when the Buddhist monks arrived in Chinese-speaking regions, they were faced with huge linguistic barriers. In order to spread Buddhism in China, they decided to translate their scriptures into Chinese. Some of the earliest notable Buddhist translators came from Gandhara,[3] Sogdiana,[4] Tocharia (northern rim of the Tarim Basin), and the eastern borderland of Parthia (located today in Iran) (Boucher, 1998). These monks translated sutras in monastic centers such as Kucha in the Tarim Basin (located today in the Xinjiang region of China) and Dunhuang (Milward, 2013: 28).

Generally speaking, translation was done through collaboration and oral transmission. Early medieval non-Chinese monks recruited teams of two to four people to translate a single text. The presiding translator, known for his erudition and firm memorization of sutras, would recite the Buddhist text orally. Depending on the presiding translator's mastery of Chinese, he would either interpret the text in Chinese himself or let his bilingual assistants explain his words in Chinese. Then, the recorder would transcribe and edit what had been interpreted into written Chinese (Cheung and Lin, 2006: 8). For example, the *Scripture of the Great Bright Enlightenment* attributed to Zhi Qian 支謙 (fl. 222–252 CE) displays enormous diversity in vocabulary and style (Nattier, 2008 [2010]), suggesting the collaborative process of the translation.[5]

A scripture can have several origin and translation versions. For instance, initially written in a dialect of the Magadha kingdom based in the eastern Ganges plain, the *Lotus Sutra* was gradually transmitted in Sanskrit and Central Asian languages northwestward into Central Asia, Nepal, the Western Region, and East Asia. The *Lotus Sutra* has had six to twelve Chinese translations. Each of the three existent Chinese translations of the *Lotus Sutra* is based on a different text, written on either palm leaves or white cotton cloth found in Khotan and Kashmir (Suwen, 2007: 16). However, these original texts may not

---

[2] Beginning in the first century BCE, the scriptures of the Theravada Buddhist canon were written in Pali. However, a later recension of the *Dhammapada* recorded in Gandhari was excavated in the Tarim Basin near Khotan.
[3] Gandhara is located in what is now northwestern Pakistan and eastern Afghanistan.
[4] Sogdiana is between the Amu Darya and the Syr Darya (rivers) in Central Asia, spread across present-day Uzbekistan, Turkmenistan, Tajikistan, Kazakhstan, and Kyrgyzstan.
[5] Zhi Qian was the disciple of Zhi Liang 支亮, who was in turn taught by Lokaksema (147–200 CE).

be in Sanskrit. They may be Iranian or Tocharian translations of Sanskrit versions (Ji, 1947; 1990; Zhu, 1992: 14).

In at least one case, a Chinese Buddhist sutra may not have had its original Sanskrit counterpart. We have the example of a Chinese Buddhist monk translating a Chinese sutra back into its supposedly original Sanskrit language. In this instance, the celebrated monk Xuanzang's "translated version" of the *Heart Sutra*, which has become the standard version in East Asia, is in fact the "original" text, created by Xuanzang himself, who extracted it from the *Perfection of Wisdom* (Prajnaparamita) in 25,000 lines. From the Chinese *Heart Sutra* he back-translated the Sanskrit *Heart Sutra* (Nattier, 1992).

Additionally, it is noteworthy that most of what we know about translation in the early medieval period consists of only a handful of names of the Central Asian Buddhist translators as the presiding translators to whom we attribute the translated texts' authorship. These include the Parthian prince An Shigao 安世高 (c. 200 BCE) and his countryman An Xuan (fl. 147 CE), the Indo-Scythian Zhi Qian, Lokaksema (Zhi Loujiachen) from the Kushan empire (fl. 147–189 CE), and Kumarajiva (c. 344–409 CE) of Indian (Kashmiri) and Tocharian parentage. These notable translators are only the tip of the iceberg of the translation community, most of whom must have already become anonymous between the Han (202 BCE–220 CE) and the Jin (266–420 CE) dynasties (Cheung and Lin, 2006).

Medieval Discourse on Translation

Buddhist translation prompted the first wave of discussions of methods and theories on what "a good translation" was in Chinese history. Zhi Qian became the first person in the history of Chinese translation to discuss translation theory. When translating and introducing Sanskrit terms, he proposed to "translate meaning" (*huiyi* 會意 or *yiyi* 意譯) rather than using the conventional method of "transcription" (*yinyi* 音譯). He suggested creating new words and phrases based upon the original Buddhist Sanskrit terms. He also advocated new ways of explaining religious jargon by adding explanatory comments to the original text. Such additions served to clarify the translated text. In the preface to the *Scripture of Dhammapada* (Figure 4), he introduced the idea of the importance of polishing the translated language and inserting interpretation into the original text to elaborate on its meaning:

> The language of Tianzhu [India] has different sounds from that of the Han empire. Their writing is called the Tian script and their language is called the Tian language [Tian also means "from Heaven"]. Their way of designating objects differs [from ours] and it is difficult to bring their meanings across [when translating]. The only early translators capable of rendering Sanskrit

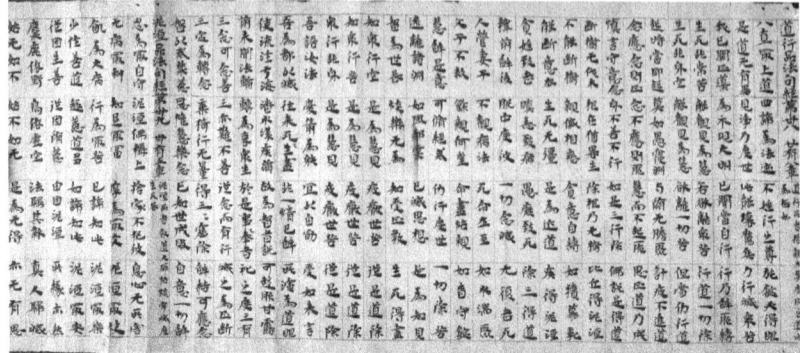

Figure 4 A segment of the manuscript *Dhammapada*, Eastern Jin dynasty, 317–420 CE (Gansu Museum, No. 001). Courtesy of Dunhuang Academy.

into Chinese while preserving the form [of the original] were the Parthian prince An Shigao, a former officer named An Xuan, and [Yan] Fotiao. Hardly anyone was capable of continuing [this work]. Later transmitters were unable to adhere so strictly [to the correct mode of the originals]; for the most part they treasured what was precious [in the Buddha's message] and expressed its main points roughly … Laozi said, "Beautiful words are not trustworthy, trustworthy words are not beautiful." Confucius stated, "Writing does not completely express speech, and speech does not completely express meanings." This shows that there was no limit to the profundity of the sages.

In this case, when communicating the Sanskrit meaning, we must do so directly and clearly. For this reason, these chants were collected and translated from the [foreign] reciters themselves. In compiling a standard text, the principle was not to add any literary adornment. When translating, if there was a passage that could not be understood, it was left out and not transmitted. There are accordingly many gaps and untranslated sections [in the *Dhammapada*]. Nonetheless, these translations, plain in wording and profound in ideas, concise in style yet broad in reference, link together the entirety of the sutras. Each section has a standard text and each sentence has its annotation. If those in India who began the study of the dharma did not study the *Dhammapada*, they were called "wanderers." The *Dhammapada* gives an auspicious entry to the beginner; it is a mysterious treasure for advanced students. It can open minds, remove doubts, persuade people, and confirm one's vocation. Studying it does not require great effort, but its fruit is vast. Should it not be called wonderful and valuable?[6] (Wei, 2016)

This passage presents the first recorded discussion of translation as a disciplined practice in Chinese history.[7] Zhi Qian emphasizes the clarity of translation as

---

[6] We thank Haun Saussy for helping with the translation.
[7] For a concise summary and analysis of Zhi Qian's biography, work, and theory of translation, see Cheung and Lin, 2006: 57–63.

paramount: An effective translation must convey meaning clearly through plain and accessible language. This approach posits the ideal translator as an eloquent communicator in the target language and a perceptive interpreter of the foreign culture. Zhi Qian advocates for the translator as an articulate mediator, ensuring Buddhist teachings could be faithfully transmitted to the Chinese audience.

Looking back at early Buddhist translation as a cross-cultural activity, some modern scholars argue that it triggered early attempts at comparative thinking through the strict third-century practice of *geyi* 格義 ("categorizing concepts"). Rather than creating a new Chinese term to designate a Buddhist concept or transcribe a foreign Buddhist term into Chinese, the translator would adopt Daoist terms to designate approximately corresponding Buddhist concepts. For example, *Dao* (the Way) was adopted as a term for bodhi, and *wuwei* (nonaction) was the term designated for nirvana (Deeg, 2008 [2010]: 83–118).[8] This recourse to the cultural and linguistic familiar no doubt occurred from time to time, but there is no conclusive evidence that it had a formative effect on the development of the terminology and ideology of Buddhism during the period of its arrival in China. In actuality, it was never put into widespread use as a practical means of translation, since the medieval Chinese thinkers were able to reason independently in the new epistemological system (Mair, 2010: 227–264; Mair, 2012: 38).

The famous translator Kumarajiva's version of the *Lotus Sutra* – one of the fundamental scriptures of Mahayana Buddhism – is a perfect example of how effective translation and independent storytelling and reasoning can be for the transmission of Buddhism to a wide range of readers. Throughout his translation, he barely uses jargon, transliteration, *geyi*, or annotation. The language of Kumarajiva's translation is plain, clear, colloquial, fluent, and free of difficult classical Chinese phrases. He and his translation committee made sure that the translation itself was compelling enough to convey the concepts in Mahayana Buddhism correctly. Kumarajiva decided to retranslate the *Lotus Sutra* because he found that his predecessor Dharmaraksa's 竺法護 (233–310) translation of the same sutra did not interpret some Buddhist concepts correctly and its language was too obscure for readers to grasp the gist of Buddhism. His translation was so successful that the monk Zhiyi 智顗 (538–597) used it as the main scripture of the Tiantai 天台 school of Chinese Buddhism of which Zhiyi was the founder (Suwen, 2007: 14–15; Lopez, 2016: 47–50). The teaching of the Tiantai school later spread to Japan and Korea.

---

[8] Max Deeg points out the rationale behind such semantic choices. Dao means "path," which relates to the Indic word *yana* which could semantically be derived from *ya-* (*yati*), "to move, to go." *Wuwei* (without action) could correspond to nirvana, which originally meant "extinguished" or "terminated" like a candle (Deeg, 2008 [2010]: 83–118).

One of the most famous parables of the *Lotus Sutra* is the burning house parable. A crumbling house is on fire. The 500 people who are living in the house are still indulging in dallying inside the house, unaware that the house is burning and that their lives are in danger. Witnessing this, their loving father outside the house fears that his children will die in the fire and finds no useful means to save them. So, he devises carriages pulled by deer, horses, and oxen and promises to give everyone a carriage. This way, he successfully convinces his children to get out of the perilous house. The following is an excerpt of an English translation based upon the sutra translated by Kumarajiva.

> Sariputra,[9] imagine that a country, or a city-state, or a municipality has a man of great power, advanced in years and of incalculable wealth, owning many fields and houses, as well as servants. His house is broad and great; it has only one doorway, but great multitudes of human beings, a hundred, or two hundred, or even five hundred, are dwelling in it. The halls are rotting, the walls crumbling, the pillars decayed at their base, the beams and ridgepoles precariously tipped. Throughout the house and all at the same time, quite suddenly a fire breaks out, burning down all the apartments. The great man's sons, ten, or twenty, or thirty of them, are still in the house.
>
> The great man, directly he sees this great fire breaking out from four directions, is alarmed and terrified. He then has this thought: "Though I was able to get out safely through this burning doorway, yet my sons within the burning house, attached as they are to their games, are unaware, ignorant, unperturbed, unafraid. The fire is coming to press in upon them, the pain will cut them to the quick. Yet at heart they are not horrified, nor have they any wish to leave."
>
> ...
>
> At that time, the great man has this thought: "This house is already aflame with a great fire. If we do not get out in time, the children and I shall certainly be burnt. I will now devise an expedient, whereby I shall enable the children to escape this disaster." The father knows the children's preconceptions, whereby each child has his preferences, his feelings being specifically attached to his several precious toys and unusual playthings.
>
> Accordingly, [the father] proclaimed to them: "The things you so love to play with are rare and hard to get. If you do not get them, you are certain to regret it later. Things like these, a variety of goat-drawn carriages, deer-drawn carriages, and ox-drawn carriages are now outside the door for you to play with. Come out of this burning house quickly, all of you! I will give all of you what you desire." The children hear what their father says. Since rare playthings are exactly what they desire, the heart of each is emboldened. Shoving one another in a mad race, altogether in a rush they leave the burning house. (Hurvitz, 1976: 58–59)

---

[9] Sariputra is a leading disciple of the Buddha. The speaker is the Buddha, and he is telling the story to Sariputra.

Kumarajiva's language is naturally fluent. He shows the clear meaning of a given passage rather than just providing a word-for-word translation (Lopez, 2016: 45). The burning house is a metaphor for the everyday desires that bring suffering to all sentient beings who are completely unaware of their misery and hence cannot transcend the mundane world. The loving father is the Buddha who, with the heart of compassion, wants to save the ordinary people from suffering. But he employs a strategy: to make "expedient devices" – the three carriages – to guide people his way. The three carriages represent the three vehicles of Buddhism expounded for the voice-hearers (Shravaka), for cause-awakened ones (pratyekabuddha), and for the bodhisattvas. At the end of the story, however, instead of giving them the three carriages promised, the father gives everyone a splendid carriage "made of the seven jewels," pulled by a white ox, "whose skin is pure white, whose bodily form is lovely, whose muscular strength is great, whose tread is even and fleet like the wind." The kids all happily ascend the splendid carriages to play, completely forgetting about the three other carriages promised to them (Hurvitz, 1976: 60). This carriage embodies Mahayana Buddhism, which can help sentient beings achieve enlightenment (Figure 5). Throughout the story, Kumarajiva barely uses transliteration, annotation, or *geyi*, except for some essential Sanskrit terms, such as *boruoboluomi* 般若波羅蜜 (Prajnaparamita), a significant concept in Mahayana Buddhism that teaches that all sentient beings possess the ability to reach enlightenment. In Kumarajiva's captivating translation and storytelling, the parable itself is powerful enough to deliver the Mahayana Buddhist message. Kumarajiva's translation has since been the most popular version up to today, widely read, annotated, and translated in East Asia and around the world.

In Buddhist translation, Sanskrit terms are still important. Xuanzang of the Tang dynasty reiterated that Sanskrit's linguistic aspects should be taken into account:

> [Sanskrit's] words are gentle and fine. Its sounds are recurrent. It either expresses many meanings with one word, or one meaning is expressed by many words. Its sound has modulation, and its tones are divided into voiced and voiceless. Since Sanskrit is so profound, its translation depends on intelligent men. Since the essence of the sutras is deep and mysterious, understanding its correct meaning relies upon people of high virtue. If the translator and his team reduce this phonetic aspect in his writing, and if they adjust the Sanskrit tones to the tones in China, the translation is not going to be good, and the translated thesis is not going to be elegant.[10]

Like Zhi Qian and Kumarajiva, Xuanzang similarly considered that the language of a good translation should be plain and clear. Yet he regarded it better, in

---

[10] We thank Max Deeg for translating the passage.

Figure 5 A mural on the burning house parable in the *Lotus Sutra*, Five Dynasties (Southern wall, Mogao Cave 98).
In the lower-right register of the painting, a household compound burns, while figures within the compound remain engrossed in riding horses or indoor activities, unaware of the fire. Some people have already exited the house. Some scramble to board the three blue-canopied carriages pulled by white oxen– vehicles symbolizing Mahayana Buddhism. Courtesy of Dunhuang Academy.

some circumstances, to transcribe the Sanskrit sounds with Chinese characters. He laid out five guidelines for transcription: do not translate the esoteric Buddhist terms; do not translate the terms that have multiple meanings; do not translate the things and deities that cannot be found in China; keep the customary transcriptions; make worshippers respect the deities and Buddhist concepts signified by these transcriptions. These five guidelines have become frequently used in the discourse of traditional Chinese translation (Cheung and Lin, 2006: 134–135).

The Impact of Buddhist Translation on the Chinese Language

Early medieval Buddhist translations greatly influenced the lexicon, grammar, and syntax of the Chinese language. As the linguist Zhu Qingzhi 朱慶之 pointed out, the term "Buddhist hybrid Chinese" refers to the language used in the Chinese translations of Buddhist scriptures and Chinese compositions on Buddhism. Buddhist hybrid Chinese contains a large number of loanwords, translation words, disyllabic words, and colloquial phrases (Zhu, 2009: 13–15). Over the span of nearly 1,000 years, between the Eastern Han (25–220 CE) and the Southern Song dynasties (1127–1279 CE), approximately 1,482 scriptures known to us today were translated into Chinese. These scriptures generated 46,000,000 Chinese characters (Zhu, 2009: 7). The sheer volume of the numerous translation projects has expanded Chinese vocabulary by as many as 35,000 words.

Some examples of loanwords include *fo* 佛 (Buddha, "the awakened"), *jie* 劫 (kalpa, "a long period of time [eon] between the creation and re-creation of a world"), *jie* 偈 (gatha, "verses"), *sanmei* 三昧 (samadhi, "the highest state of mental concentration"), *niepan* 涅槃 or *nihuan* 泥洹 (nirvana, "the transcendence beyond suffering and the cycle of death and rebirth"). In terms of translated words, for instance, we find examples such as *rulai* 如來 (tathagata), *falun* 法輪 (Dharmacakra), *mo* 魔 (mara), *cibei* 慈悲 ("compassion"; *karuna*), *jietuo* 解脫 ("liberation"; *moksha*), *yinyuan* 因緣 (karma), *shijie* 世界 ("universe"; lokadhatu), *lunhui* 輪迴 ("reincarnation"; *samsara*), and *fanbai* 梵呗 ("hymns"; Brahma-patha).

Aside from coining new terms and phrases, another method of translation and transcription is to borrow existing Chinese phrases and designate a new Buddhist meaning for them. For instance, *yingxiang* 影響 ("influence" in modern Chinese) originally meant "shadow and sound." But later translators adopted the word to signify emptiness and karma in Buddhism (Zhu, 1992: 231–234). Another example is *ayi* 阿姨 which in Chinese means "aunt," but in Buddhist translation it is used to designate the Sanskrit term *upasika* 優婆夷, a common title for women of high social status who believe in Buddhism and still live at home. Further, *jiehui* 節會 in Chinese indicates "a festival" or a "gathering of people to celebrate a festival." But when used in Buddhist translation, it designates an Indian festival that takes place before New Year's Day. *Zuxingzi* 族姓子 originally meant a son of a family clan in Chinese, but in Buddhist translation it is used to designate the Sanskrit term *kulaputra*, meaning a noble-born son (Zhu, 2010).

Further, Buddhist hybrid Chinese consists of a large number of disyllabic words, rapidly expanding the disyllabic and multisyllabic vocabulary of the Medieval Chinese language. One major reason is that the Buddhist scriptures are meant for memorization and oral recitation. Regular rhythm that facilitates easy memorization then leads to the creation of numerous disyllabic and multisyllabic words in Buddhist scriptures (Zhu, 1992: 124–129).

In terms of grammar, Buddhist translation also integrates Sanskrit grammar into certain Chinese phrases. An obvious example is *rushi wowen* 如是我聞 (Skt: *Evam maya-srutam*) which in English means "Thus have I heard." The Chinese word order imitates the Sanskrit grammatical formula. If the translation were in Chinese word order, it would have been 我聞如是. Before the fifth century CE, the entire Chinese translation of the Indic Buddhist phrase was *wen rushi* 聞如是 without the first-person pronoun. The term *rushi wowen* 如是我聞 is a highly exceptional phrase that imitates Indic grammatical order and could have resulted from the different practices of diverse translation schools (Nattier, 2013).

The adoption of vernacular language rather than classical Chinese in Buddhist scripture translation may have been due to philosophical, religious, and realistic reasons. First, language is an *upaya* or convenient means for the zealous Buddhist monks to spread their faith so as to rescue all sentient beings from suffering in samsara. Ultimately, language is unimportant in Buddhism: The *Suttanipata* considers the Buddha beyond language. In the *Theragatha*, the Buddha cannot be sensed in language or sound (Gómez, 1977: 446a), and in Mahayana Buddhism, speech can obstruct the spread of the Way. Chan Buddhism further emphasizes the unimportance of language and abides by the rule of transmitting the dharma through the mind rather than through texts.

Second, significantly and in reality, since early Buddhist translators all came from South Asia and Central Asia, Chinese was not their mother tongue. They gradually learned colloquial Chinese through everyday experiences. As a result, when they interpreted the scriptures orally in front of the recorder, they naturally used many colloquial expressions which were then jotted down by the recorder and incorporated into the Chinese translation. This interesting oral–written translation process gave rise to the Chinese written vernacular language which was largely excluded in the discourses of Chinese classics, historiography, and classical poetry (Mair, 1994a).

Concluding Remarks

Translation is a prime example of how literary diffusion takes place. Buddhist scripture translation brought into Chinese language a plethora of Sanskrit terms and Buddhist ideas through transliteration and translation. Such diffusion dramatically expanded Chinese vocabulary and left a mark on Chinese grammar and syntax; most significantly, it hastened the emergence of written vernacular Chinese. Its profound influence on the Chinese language has been long-lasting. Through lucid and effective translation, coordinated by visionary translators such as Zhi Qian, Kumarajiva, and Xuanzang, many Buddhist tales like the burning house allegory have inspired and influenced generations of Chinese monks, nuns, laymen, and laywomen for centuries. These tales continued to transcend borders to spread to other countries and cultures. Buddhist scripture translation also sparked early discussion of methods and theories on what constituted a "good" translation. These early medieval dialogues herald the cross-cultural comparative thinking and translingual practice widely discussed in today's global context.

2 *Bianwen* ("Transformation Texts") and Their Importance

Besides Chinese language and cultural discourses, Buddhist literary diffusion created new genres of Chinese literature. Arguably one of the most important sources for understanding the development of Chinese literature, *bianwen* ("transformation texts"), a genre of lay Buddhist storytelling, is a case in point. However, nothing was known about *bianwen* ("transformation texts") before the beginning of the twentieth century: For 1,000 years, from the early eleventh century to the end of the nineteenth century, the manuscripts on which they were written lay sealed inside a cave outside Dunhuang. The chief glories of Buddhist art (wall paintings and sculptures) at Dunhuang are to be found in the Mogao Caves, sixteen miles southeast of the town. The Mogao Caves are a complex of about 500 temples and shrines built into a cliff face of soft conglomerate. One of them, Cave 17, constitutes a small library that served as a repository for approximately 60,000 manuscripts that are now known as the Dunhuang manuscripts. The story of how, when, and why the manuscripts were deposited and sealed in Cave 17, who discovered them a millennium later, their contents, and the way they were distributed around the world is a separate and very complicated tale (Hao, 2020). Two of the key figures in the exploration and early investigation of these Dunhuang manuscripts were the Hungarian-British archaeologist Marc Aurel Stein (1862–1943) and the French philologist Paul Pelliot (1878–1945). The manuscripts they retrieved from Cave 17 were taken back to England and France where they were accessioned in the British Library and Bibliothèque nationale, respectively, and ordered under the manuscript numbers preceded by "S" (Stein) and "P" (Pelliot).

The vast majority of the Dunhuang manuscripts are sutras and other Buddhist religious texts, but there are also Confucian and Daoist works, classics, histories, medical and mathematical treatises, contracts and other legal documents, dictionaries, music scores, geographical and astronomical maps and discourses, plus records and accounts dealing with virtually all other realms of human thought and activity. They are written in a range of languages (Khotanese and Sogdian [Middle Iranian], Tibetan, Sanskrit, Tangut, Old Uighur, and others), though naturally most are in Chinese. For the purposes of this section, the most vital subset of the Dunhuang manuscripts is a group of between roughly 200 and 800 manuscripts (depending on how they are classified and counted), the content of which may be described as popular literature.

The popular literary works from Dunhuang consist of a variety of poetry, prose, prosimetra, and other genres. Among the more noteworthy genres of such Dunhuang popular literature are lyrics (*quzici*), ballads and songs (*geci*), folk rhapsodies (*fu*), "seat-settling texts" (*yazuowen*), sutra lectures (*jiangjingwen*; Sen and Mair, 2005), expositions of karma (*yinyuan, yuanqi*), and the like (Schmid, 2001).[11] Unfortunately, for the accurate description and classification of Dunhuang popular literary genres, these and many other forms of popular literature found in the cache of manuscripts in the library in Cave 17 are usually lumped under the broad rubric of *bianwen*.

Within the subset of Dunhuang popular literature, the most vital genre for comprehending the overall development of Chinese literature is that of the transformation texts or *bianwen*. Since the name of the genre is not immediately transparent, it is necessary to understand what "transformation" means in this context. This is by no means an easy task, and in the first fifty or more years after the discovery of the Dunhuang manuscripts, scholars wrestled over a plethora of interpretations of the term. Some said that it indicated the alternation between sung and spoken portions of prosimetric texts (formerly called "chantefables"), while others argued that it signified the change from the classical/literary language to vernacular language, and there were countless other speculations about its meaning.

Because there was no agreement on precisely what *bian* meant or what constituted *bianwen*, there was wild disagreement until the 1970s over how many *bianwen* there were, with guesstimates ranging from about 80 to 800. (One scholar, who shall remain nameless, even hazarded that there were 8,000!) Given the chaotic situation with regard to the nature of the genre and the numbers, in order to bring a semblance of order to the field of *bianwen* studies, it was necessary to carefully examine the entire corpus of Dunhuang popular literature and establish criteria that were based on the extant manuscripts that actually bore the designation *bian* or *bianwen* in their title. When all of the manuscripts of Dunhuang popular literature (*su wenxue*) were subjected to this rigorous test, it turned out that there were no more than twenty-eight texts with twelve stories represented (due to multiple manuscripts for some of the stories). Based on a still narrower set of criteria, there are only seven stories represented

---

[11] For a diverse selection of Dunhuang popular literary genres, expertly – though not always completely – translated into English, see Waley (1960).

in the *bianwen* corpus. However, since there are multiple copies of several of these stories, the total is eighteen to twenty-one extant *bianwen* manuscripts (Mair, 1989b; chapter 2).

The fundamental identifying characteristics of *bianwen* in the narrow sense comprise

1. a unique verse-introductory formula ("Here is the place where X happened. How shall I describe it?"; cf. the verse-introductory formula of karmic narratives: "This is the time when X happened. What did they say?");
2. an implicit or explicit relationship to the illustrations, correlating to the verse-introductory formula, where the "place" refers to a scene depicted in the painting that was used as a storytelling aid by the performer;
3. an episodic narrative progression;
4. the homogeneity of language, with a conspicuously greater usage of the vernacular and colloquial language than in typical contemporary writing; and
5. a prosimetric structure in which the text alternates between spoken (prose) and poetic or metrical (sung or cantillated) passages.

These are the seven *bianwen* stories based on these five characteristics:

1. "The Transformation Text on Mahamaudgalyayana's Rescue of His Mother from the Dark Regions." The main manuscript is S2614, but there are eight other copies. The hero's name in Chinese is Mulian. Relying on the power of the Buddha, he helps his mother escape from hell. This tale is celebrated in later Chinese literature for its evocation of filial piety.
2. "The Transformation Text on the Subjugation of Demons." This is found in S5511 and two other manuscripts, including the uniquely precious P4524, the only surviving illustrated *bian* storytelling scroll. This *bianwen* relates the contest of supernatural powers between Śariputra (one of the Buddha's chief disciples, who is often paired with Mahamaudgalyayana or Mulian), and Raudraksa, chief of the six heretical masters.
3. "The Transformation on the Han General, Wang Ling." This is written on S5437 and two other manuscripts. The basis for this tale is a brief account of approximately eighty characters extracted from the biography of Wang Ling in fascicle 40 of the *History of the Han Dynasty* (*Han shu*: 40). The author of the transformation text has expanded this into a story that is approximately fifty times the length of the original. It relates how the Chu armies of Xiang Yu repeatedly defeated the Han armies of Liu Bang, leading Wang Ling and his associate, Guan Ying, to make a surprise attack on the enemy camp.

A major focus of the story is on the brave, sacrificial role that Wang Ling's mother plays in encouraging her son in his resolve.

4. [A Transformation Text on Wang Zhaojun; title missing on manuscript]. P2553. This is a version of a very popular legend with a historical basis (*History of the Han Dynasty*, 9). The heroine is one of the four famous beauties of ancient China. She is married off to a Hun chieftain as a "peace bride." Along the way, seated on a horse, she plays sorrowful melodies on a balloon lute (*pipa*) – a poignant scene in the sorrowful tale about her that was often recounted in poems, stories, and dramas, both before and after the *bianwen* was written.

5. [A Transformation Text on Li Ling; title missing on manuscript]. The manuscript is preserved in the collection of the National Library of China. This heartrending story of General Li Ling's surrender to the Huns is ultimately derived from the well-known accounts in the *Records of the Grand Historian* (*Shiji*: 109) by Sima Qian (145–c. 86 BCE), who was directly involved in the original events, and the *History of the Han Dynasty* (54). Li Ling's captivity among the Huns was a favorite topic of the Dunhuang authors and was written up in other forms beside the transformation text.

6. [A Transformation Text on Zhang Yichao; title missing on manuscript]. P2962. A vivid, contemporaneous tale of a local hero, this fragmentary account relates the expulsion of the Tibetans from the area around Dunhuang. Scenes from these events are depicted in the wall paintings at the Mogao Caves.

7. [A Transformation Text on Zhang Huaishen; title missing on manuscript]. P3451. Another contemporaneous tale of a local hero, this fragmentary account relates the achievements of Zhang Huaishen, the nephew of Zhang Yichao and his successor as the leader of the Returning to Righteousness Army. Like the Zhang Yichao transformation text, it emphasizes the fighting spirit of the Chinese troops and their valor in battle.

Just from this list of genuine *bianwen*, it can be seen that the genre – as might well be expected – started with Buddhist tales, since the overall form and language were heavily indebted to Buddhist sources; the form and language were then applied to Chinese historical records and eventually used in local, contemporaneous accounts. For example, the following is a passage from "The Transformation Text on Mahamaudgalyayana's Rescue of His Mother from the Dark Regions."

This is the place where Maudgalyayana is led in by the gatekeepers to see the Great King who asks him his business:

When the Great King saw Maudgalyayana enter,
He quickly joined his palms in salutation and was about to stand up:
"What is your reason for coming here, reverend sir?"
Hurriedly, he bowed respectfully from behind his table.
"Your coming here embarrasses me, oh Exemplar!
I, your disciple, am situated here in this infernal region,
Where I flog sinners to determine whether they shall remain dead or be reborn;
Although I do not recognize you, reverend sir,
It was long ago that I had heard of your name.
. . .
That I, poor monk, had a father and mother who, when alive,
Day and night observed the laws of abstinence, never eating after noon?
Based on their behavior while in the World of Mankind,
After their deaths, they should have been reborn in the Pure Land.
My father alone is dwelling in the mansions of heaven,
But I cannot locate my dear mother in any of the heavens;
In my estimation, she should not even have passed through hell,
My only fear is that she may have been unjustly punished by High Heaven.
I have followed her traces to the edges of heaven and earth,
Filled with sorrowful vexation, I heave a long sigh;
If she has come to this realm because of her karmic retribution,
Perhaps you, oh Great King, would have been made aware of it."

When Maudgalyayana had finished speaking, the Great King then summoned him to the upper part of the hall. There he was given audience with Ksitigarbha Bodhisattva to whom he quickly paid obeisance (Mair, 1994b: 1100–1101).

The above-cited passage clearly shows the generic features of a *bianwen*. The passage begins with a unique introductory verse formula "This is the place where . . ." indicating that this "place" is represented in a scene depicted in the illustrated storytelling scroll. The alteration between the verse (sung) and the prose (spoken) is typical of the prosimetric structure of a *bianwen*. Further, the passage contains quite a few vernacular phrases, such as 既見 (when . . . saw), 連忙 (hurriedly), 雖然 (although), 被 (passive tense), and 便 (then) (Figure 6).

With this general understanding of the corpus and nature of *bianwen*, returning to the meaning of *bian* ("transformation") is essential because it was confusion over that which troubled the study of the genre from the very beginning in the first half of the twentieth century. Perhaps the best way to approach the challenge of exactly what the *bian* in *bianwen* signifies is to point out that Monkey, in *Journey to the West*, possesses seventy-two (a magic number) miraculous *bian* ("transformations") that he uses to outwit his opponents. In the "Transformation Text on the Subjugation of Demons," Sariputra produces the same kind of transformations, using his prodigious mental powers produced through deep, intense meditation.

Figure 6 Scene of gruesome tortures in hell from the Five Dynasties (907–979) Maudgalyayana transformation wall painting in Mogao Cave 19 at Dunhuang. The monk in white robe is Maudgalyayana. The writing in the vertical cartouche is Old Uyghur and it says: "On a day of the first 10 day period (旬), the fifth month of the Year of the Snake, we two, Sangadas(?) and Birmese, came to this mountain temple, burned incense, and prayed for the cleansing of all our misdeeds! Then we rose, scattered flowers, and bowed before returning to Aqbaliq. Thus I, Birmese, have written this."
Courtesy of Dunhuang Academy.

This is graphically depicted in P4524, the illustrated *bian* storytelling scroll (Figure 7). Employed by the likes of Sariputra and Monkey, such transformations can be thought of as "mind-emanations."

Bianwen are based on *nirmana* ("metamorphosis"), a core concept in Mahayana ("Great Vehicle") Buddhism. It is quite in keeping with Buddhist ontology to say that an adept created, made, or produced something (a manifestation) through transformation. It is also common in Buddhist thought and literature to speak of supernatural or magical creations produced through transformation.

Stepping back a bit from such rarefied philosophical notions, for those who are interested in genre studies, the available historical evidence indicates that the performers of *bian* ("transformations") made their living by reciting them on the street and were chiefly, if not exclusively, women (Mair, 1989b: chapter 5). As for the history and sociolinguistics of "ancient Chinese books," a curious feature of *bianwen* is that, to the extent that it can be determined, the scribes and copyists responsible for the manuscripts that have come down to us were "lay students" (*xueshilang*) who studied a comprehensive curriculum in the monastery schools at Dunhuang (Mair, 1981).

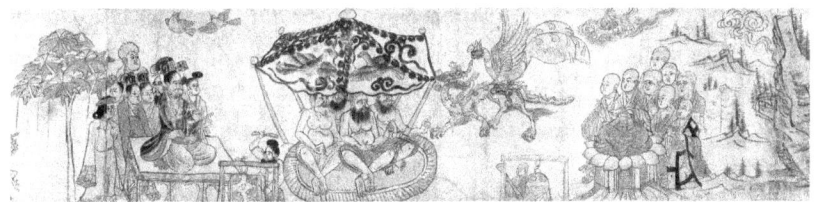

Figure 7 A segment of the pictorial scroll of the *Transformation Text of Conquering Demons*, portraying the magical combat between Sariputra and Raudraksa. Courtesy of Bibliothèque nationale de France.

Finally, the degree to which *bianwen* are intimately bound to illustrations cannot be overemphasized. As we have seen, the *bian* in *bianwen* quite literally signifies an image or scene that has been manifested through transformation. A close contemporary corollary of *bianwen* are *bianxiang* ("transformation tableaux") or narrative wall paintings (Mair, 1986). We cannot, however, directly equate the stories presented in *bianwen* with those portrayed in *bianxiang*, since the latter are more overtly Buddhist and scripturally based, whereas the former are more of a folk-type and were dependent upon oral transmission.

The connection with illustrations is further exemplified in *pinghua* ("expository tales" or "plain texts") of the Song (960–1279) and Ming (1368–1644) periods, where the upper register of each page is occupied by an illustration of what is going on in the written story at that point. It is as though a picture scroll, such as that employed by the Sariputra picture storyteller, were unrolled and spread out at the top of the page. Such illustrations are a feature of much published fiction during the second millennium CE.

The international dimensions of this type of picture storytelling, whose roots can be traced back to Indian folk literature and art, are evident, for example, in Indonesian/Javanese *wayang kulit* which is picture storytelling with a scroll, but it is also a clear predecessor of other types of dramatic performance, including the famous puppet theater and shadow play of Indonesia/Java. This connection of Song-Ming *pinghua* and Tang dynasty *bian* storytelling with picture scrolls is evidenced by the records of a Chinese traveler to Indonesia who went with Admiral Zheng He (1371–1433/35) as his secretary: He observed that *wayang beber* picture storytelling was "just like our *pinghua* back home" (Mair, 1988: chapter 3).

Although preserved in manuscripts only in the remote, desert town of Dunhuang, *bianwen* ("transformation texts") had an enormous impact on later Chinese popular literature, especially fiction and drama. Dating to the Tang (618–907) and Five Dynasties (907–979) periods as living oral performance texts, these works of popular literature were found in the East Asian heartland as well. Yet we knew of their existence only through rare, scattered historical and anecdotal records that were not recognized for what they signified before the discovery and investigation of the actual *bianwen* manuscripts from Dunhuang.

Concluding Remarks

Bianwen is an excellent example of how Buddhist literary diffusion gave rise to new literary genres and art forms in China. In response to the question of what *bianwen* is, we can say that *bianwen* was a revolutionary medieval genre of popular literature that bequeathed much to the Chinese popular literary and performance tradition, including the ubiquitous prosimetric form of fiction and drama, the fondness for narrative illustrations, and the legitimization of vernacular language (Mair, 1994b). While *bianwen* were not composed exclusively in the vernacular language, they did use a considerable component of language that was neither classical nor literary. As such, it is fair to say that *bianwen* were the first narrative texts in the history of Chinese literature that included a relatively large amount of vernacularisms, both grammatically and lexically. While sooner or later, the Chinese would have begun to write closer to the way they spoke than to the book language of the typical classical/literary style that had been employed by a minuscule number of literate individuals in pre-Tang times extending all the way back to the beginning of the script in the Shang era (ca. 1600–1046 BCE), there is no doubt that the Buddhist-inspired *bianwen* hastened the actualization of vernacular writing. Were it not for the chance preservation and miraculous discovery of the Dunhuang manuscripts in the desert frontier of Gansu, much of the true history of the development of Chinese literature might have remained unknown forever.

3 Buddhism, the Literary World, and the "Journey to the West" Stories

India–China Buddhist literary diffusion has profoundly influenced the literary world of Chinese literature. A notable example is the "journey to the West" stories that recount the pilgrimage to India by the legendary Tang monk Xuanzang 玄奘 (602–664, also known by his honorific, Tripitaka 三藏). Xuanzang spent seventeen years in his travels to India to bring the Buddhist scriptures to China (see Figure A3 in the Appendix and the online resources). His heroic journey has given rise to many legends, folklore accounts, stories, performances, and visual arts depicting his pilgrimage.[12] Influenced by Valmiki's celebrated third-century

---

[12] Xuanzang's hagiographies laid the foundation for the mythologization of his journey (Akira, 1993: 53). Tang emperor Taizong endorsed his great achievements after he returned to China by appointing him the first presiding abbot of the Giant Wild Goose Pagoda, making Xuanzang the

BCE Hindu epic *Ramayana* and Buddhism, the fictive accounts on world travel produced between the Tang dynasty and Yuan dynasty (1271–1368) eventually paved the way for the composition and publication of *Journey to the West* (Xiyou ji 西遊記, 1592), by Wu Cheng'en – one of the four masterpieces of the Ming dynasty (1368–1644). The novel has since continuously inspired new literature, art, film, television series, plays, cartoons, computer games, not just in China but throughout East Asia and globally from premodern to modern times (Figures 8–10).[13] Doubtlessly, Xuanzang's legendary pilgrimage will continue to stimulate people to tell his timeless tale in countless ways in the future. The "journey to the west" narratives embody early global influences, Buddhist literary diffusion, and modern globalization. Particularly, *Journey to the West*, like the *Ramayana*, stands as a widely recognized representative of world literature.[14]

To show that early globalism and Buddhist literary diffusion have influenced the literary world of "journey to the West" stories, this section will begin by examining the *Ramayana*'s transmission to China and the appearance of the monkey disciple in the "journey to the West" stories after 1000 CE. Then, this section will sketch out the cross-cultural reception of a few important Buddhist deities and schools in China that shape the literary landscape of the "journey to the West" stories. Finally, this section will discuss the Buddhist tropes of magical battles and karmic retribution as integral to the narrative structure of the stories. Overall, this section will look at how Buddhism has impacted the literary world of the "journey to the West" stories, and to a large extent, Chinese literature.

Among the many oral, textual, and visual depictions of Xuanzang's journey, notable texts that clearly show Buddhist influence include the earliest known

---

most famous of all Chinese Buddhist monks who traveled to India (Beal, 1884; Li, 1995b). In 672, Taizong also composed an epitaph titled "The Emperor's Preface to the Sacred Teaching of the Buddhist Canon Tripitaka," praising Xuanzang and his achievements, and had it inscribed on the monument erected at the five-story pagoda that enshrined Xuanzang's bones at the Xingjiao Monastery near Chang'an. In 688, the monks Huili (615 c. 677) and Yanzong (fl. 688) composed *The Biography of Tripitaka Dharma Master of the Great Imperial Favor Temple*. The Japanese also honored Xuanzang. In the Kamakura period (1185–1333), a Japanese artist created for the Kofuku-ji temple in Nara a set of twelve picture scrolls titled *Genjo sanzo e* that illustrate the events of Xuanzang's life based upon his Chinese biographies (Wong, 2002).

[13] Some notable adaptations include the Japanese TV show *Saiyūki* (1978–1980), the popular Japanese manga *Dragon Ball* series (1984–1995), the Hong Kong fantasy-comedy film *A Chinese Odyssey* (1995) starring Stephen Chow, Gene Luen Yang's graphic novel *American Born Chinese* (2006), the Chinese-American fantasy-adventure martial arts film *The Forbidden Kingdom* (2008) featuring Jet Li as Sun Wukong, the stage musical *Monkey: Journey to the West* (2007) by the New York-based theatre and film director Chen Shi-Zheng, accompanied by the British artist Jamie Hewlett's fantastical artworks on the same theme, and the recent action role-playing 3D computer game *Black Myth: Wukong* which went viral online upon its release by Game Science in August 2024. For a discussion of modern cross-cultural adaptations of the *Journey to the West*, see Sun (2018).

[14] Goethe saw that "world literature" (*Weltliteratur*) had the ability to generate mutual understanding and tolerance across cultures (Cheah, 2008: 26–38).

Figure 8 Portrait of Tripitaka, Kamakura Period of Japan (1185–1333). Courtesy of the National Museum of Japan.

written version of the "journey to the West" story (the Kōzanji version) – the *shihua* (tale interspersed with poems) text titled *The Story of How the Monk of the Great Country of Tang Brought Back the Sutras* (hereafter *The Story of the Monk*); a play that was popular in the Song and the Yuan dynasties titled *The River-Floating Monk Chen Guangrui*; an episode about a dragon king recorded in the Ming encyclopedia commissioned by the Yongle emperor (r. 1402–1424); three Yuan dynasty plays – *The Three Transformations of Fierce Nata*, *The Wild Ape Listening to the Sutra Chanting at Mount Longji* (hereafter *The Wild Ape*), and the twenty-four-act *Journey to the West* variety drama (hereafter *Journey Drama 24*), as well as the Ming novel *Journey to the West* first published in 1592 (Dudbridge, 1970).

From Hanuman to Monkey King: The Diffusion of the *Ramayana* in China

The Monkey from the "journey to the West" stories arguably bears a profound similarity to the simian god Hanuman in the *Ramayana*. Let us see how similar they are. The following passage from the *Ramayana* tells us that Hanuman takes a leap over the ocean to Lanka, by shapeshifting to the size of a mountain, to rescue Rama's abducted wife Sita:

Early Globalism and Chinese Literature 27

Figure 9 Jade Rabbit and Sun Wukong, from the series *One Hundred Aspects of the Moon*, by Tsukioka Yoshitoshi (1839–1892). Wikipedia Commons.

Cupping his hands in reverence to the sun god Surya, great Indra, the wind god Pavana, self-existent Brahma, and all the great beings, he resolved to set forth. Facing east, the clever monkey cupped his hands in reverence to his father Pavana and then began to increase his size in preparation for his journey to the south. Thus, the monkey formed his resolution to jump. In order to fulfill Rama's purpose, he increased in size – right before the eyes of the monkey leaders – as does the sea on the days of spring tide. In his desire to leap the ocean, he assumed a body of immeasurable size and pressed down on the mountain with his fore and hind feet.

...

So great was his speed that as he leapt up, the trees that grew on the mountain flew up after him on every side with all their branches pressed flat. And so he leapt up into the clear sky, and the force of his haunches was such that he carried with him the trees full of blossoms and love-maddened *koyastibhakas*. (Goldman, 2021: 429–430)

Figure 10 A poster of the Hong Kong fantasy-comedy film *A Chinese Odyssey* (1995) that is loosely based upon the plot of *Journey to the West*. Wikipedia Commons.

The following passage from the *Journey to the West* relates that Monkey King takes a leap across the palm of the Tathagata Buddha on a bet that if Monkey can somersault out of the hand of the Buddha, the Buddha will allow him to replace the Jade Emperor to rule the Celestial Palace:

> When the Great Sage heard this, he said to himself, snickering, "What a fool this Tathagata is! A single somersault of mine can carry old Monkey a hundred and eight thousand miles, yet his palm is not even one foot across. How could I possibly not jump clear of it?" He asked quickly, "You're certain that your decision will stand?" "Certainly it will," said Tathagata. He stretched out his right hand, which was about the size of a lotus leaf. Our Great Sage put away his compliant rod and, summoning his power, leaped up and stood right in the center of the Patriarch's hand. He said simply, "I'm off!" and he was gone – all but invisible like a streak of light in the clouds. Training the eye of wisdom on him, the Buddhist Patriarch saw that the Monkey King was hurtling along relentlessly like a whirligig.
>
> As the Great Sage advanced, he suddenly saw five flesh-pink pillars supporting a mass of green air. "This must be the end of the road," he said. "When

I go back presently, Tathagata will be my witness and I shall certainly take up residence in the Palace of Divine Mists." But he thought to himself, "Wait a moment! I'd better leave some kind of memento if I'm going to negotiate with Tathagata." He plucked a hair and blew a mouthful of magic breath onto it, crying, "Change!" It changed into a writing brush with extra thick hair soaked in heavy ink. On the middle pillar he then wrote in large letters the following line: "The Great Sage, Equal to Heaven, has made a tour of this place." When he had finished writing, he retrieved his hair, and with a total lack of respect he left a bubbling pool of monkey urine at the base of the first pillar. He reversed his cloud-somersault and went back to where he had started. Standing on Tathagata's palm, he said, "I left, and now I'm back. Tell the Jade Emperor to give me the Celestial Palace." (Yu, 2012: vol. 1, 194–195)

These two excerpts show that both Monkey and Hanuman share the ability to cloud-soar. Like Hanuman, Monkey can also shapeshift. In fact, he has seventy-two transformations. They both played the role of counselor: Hanuman serves Rama to help him find his wife Sita. Monkey assists Tripitaka to reach India.[15] But while Hanuman appears majestic and heroic, Monkey is often depicted as crafty, sneaky, and even ugly-looking. Moreover, Monkey is mischievous. Leaving urine on the palm of the Buddha is a typical example of his naughty and unruly character. After all, *Journey to the West* is a humorous book. Nonetheless, the commonalities between Hanuman and Monkey have naturally led scholars to speculate on the *Ramayana*'s transmission to China and Indian influence on Chinese literature.

Indeed, even though the *Ramayana* is long, its episodes were introduced into China in a piecemeal fashion. These episodic tales were continuously referenced, paraphrased, and retold in many medieval Chinese Buddhist texts translated from Indic sutras. Here we only give two of the most significant examples. In 247 CE, Seng Hui 僧會, a monk of Sogdian background, arrived in Nanjing and translated the *Sat-paramita-samgraha-Sutra* (*Sutra of the Collection of the Six Perfections* 六度集經) into Chinese. The forty-sixth story in this collection titled "Jataka of an Unnamed King" is a miniature version of the *Ramayana*. It tells the story of a bodhisattva who is a respected sovereign of his country. His uncle, ruling a different country, is, however, a greedy and ruthless man. The uncle plans to conquer the kingdom of the bodhisattva. He eventually takes over the kingdom, and the bodhisattva and his wife seek shelter in the forests. An evil dragon living in the ocean covets the bodhisattva's beautiful wife and abducts her. A giant bird comes to the rescue to fight with the dragon. The king climbs mountains to look for his wife and encounters a sorrowful giant ape who divulges to him that his monkey troops

---

[15] For a more detailed and thorough comparison of Hanuman and Monkey, see Walker (1998).

were taken away by the king's uncle. The ape helps the king to defeat his uncle and he regains his monkey troops. Afterward, the monkeys help the king to rescue his wife from the evil dragon. The uncle dies without a child to succeed to his throne and the bodhisattva is welcomed back to be the king. The wife also proved her chastity and loyalty to the king while she was being held prisoner.

Further, in 472 CE, Kimkarya (or Kekaya, Ji Jiaye 吉迦夜), working with the Chinese Sramana Tan Yao 曇耀, translated *Dasarata-nidana* (*The Tale of the Origin of the "King of Ten Luxuries"* 十奢王緣) as the first entry in the *Saṃyukta Ratnapiṭaka Sūtra* (*Sutra of Miscellaneous Jewels* 雜寶藏經). The story tells of a king named Ten Luxuries who has four wives, each of whom has a son. Ten Luxuries makes one of his sons, Rama, the crown prince. But his youngest wife schemes to make the king appoint her son, Poluotuo 婆羅陀, the crown prince. Rama is subsequently banished to the forest for twelve years. After the death of the king, the conscientious Poluotuo criticizes his selfish mother and seeks his brother in the forest to persuade him to return to the palace to succeed their father. Upon being repeatedly rejected, Poluotuo then takes one of Rama's shoes back and places it on the throne as if Rama were sitting there acting as the sovereign. After Rama finishes his exile, he returns to the palace and eventually accepts his younger brother's constant requests to be the king. Because the two brothers are filial to their father and loyal to each other, the kingdom is blessed with a bountiful harvest every year and the people are all wealthy, healthy, and happy (Ji, 1991: 207–208).

Together, these two Chinese texts fully translate the storyline of the *Ramayana* into Chinese, although the stories are instilled with Chinese values such as filial piety and loyalty. While the oral versions are inevitably much longer and detailed, the Chinese versions are similar to all other non-Indian written versions in terms of detail and length (Ji, 1991: 208–216). As a result, the stories in the *Ramayana* spread among monks and laymen, along with the widely circulated sutras.

In fact, Buddhist scriptures contain a large number of folk tales. These humorous stories, clever parables, and moral tales are short and simple, hence easy to remember and spread orally rather than by paper and ink. For example, the *Jatakas* are a collection of 500 folk stories, parables, and fairy tales that tell the life story of Shakyamuni (Ji, 1991: 134–135).

There could be multiple global–regional sources of the *Ramayana* that influenced its transmission in China. We cannot overlook the considerable possibility that the *Ramayana*, the stories about Hanuman and the cult of monkeys, were transmitted from Southeast Asia. In the first place, the use of Sanskrit was widespread in Southeast Asia beginning in the fifth century. From Indonesia to Cambodia to Thailand, theatrical and ritual performances of the *Ramayana* took place frequently in cities and towns in literally every country in Southeast Asia.

Figure 11 A bas-relief portraying Hanuman in the *Ramayana* (The Prambanan Temple in Java). Photograph by Yuanfei Wang.

By the early tenth century, there was already an old Javanese *Ramayana*, based on the *Bhatti-kavya* (*Ravanavadha of Bhatti*) which tells the Indian epic story while illuminating Sanskrit grammar. Since then, more than 200 versions of the *Ramayana* have been found in Indonesia (Mair, 1989a: 670). Stone inscriptions from Prasat Ba An of Cambodia and the bas-reliefs at Angor Wat in Cambodia, Wat Phra Jetubon in Bangkok, and Indonesia's Panataran and Prambanan all demonstrate the strong currency of the *Ramayana* and Hanuman in Southeast Asia (Figure 11). In Thailand, although the country's historical archives were lost in the fire that destroyed the Ayutthaya kingdom (1351–1767) set by the Burmese in 1767, the Thai *Ramayana* was composed on the order of King Rama I (1782–1809) in an effort to reconstruct the history of Siam (Kasetsiri, 1976: 54). A dozen story scenes, motifs, and archetypes, most of which come from the Laotian *Gvay Dvorabhi*, concern Hanuman. They are surprisingly like the Monkey King. Noteworthily, *Gvay Dvorabhi* was orally disseminated (Mair, 1989a: 697).

In the second place, the *Ramayana* was also widely known among the ethnic peoples living on the borderlands of China. For instance, the Thai-speaking Dai people living in Yunnan province, a region bordering Burma, have had many versions of the Dai language translation of the *Ramayana*. The Dai language is in the same language family of Thai spoken by the majority of the people of Thailand so the Dai people likely received the Hindu epic from Thailand or

Burma. Further, in Tibet, Mongolia, and Xinjiang, archaeologists have found manuscripts translated from the *Ramayana* story in Tibetan, Mongolian, ancient Khotanese, and the Tocharian languages (Ji, 1991: 218–238).

In *The Year 1000: When Explorers Connected the World – and Globalization Began*, the historian Valerie Hansen proposes that 1000 CE was the year when "globalization" – as Hansen puts it – truly began, starting with "Viking" explorers' journeys across the North Atlantic to Greenland and Canada – a voyage that closed that particular global loop for the first time (Hansen, 2020: 25). In China, the Song and Liao (916–1125) emperors signed the Treaty of Chanyuan in 1005 to establish a century-old agreement that suited both sides. While the Liao in the north turned to the Steppe, forming a cross-regional land route along the Silk Road, the restricted borders forced the Song in the south to explore overseas connections through Southeast Asia. As a result, the coastal cities in the South thrived. Quanzhou, for instance, a port city in Fujian, became one of the most flourishing cities in the world (Hansen, 2020: 23, 158).

After the year 1000, a robust transregional Buddhist network in north Asia came into shape. The land and sea trade routes increased the transmission of Buddhism in northern and southern China. Nomadic polities such as the Khotan, Khitan Liao, and Tangut Xia, as well as the Chinese polities of the Northern and Southern Song all promoted Buddhism. As a result, Buddhist temples, pagodas, and murals thrived (Figure 12).

This thriving Buddhist network brought to China more stories of Hanuman and the *Ramayana* from India and Southeast Asia than before. Murals and

Figure 12 The 6.7-meter-long bas-reliefs carved during the Song dynasties, from Hangzhou's Lingyin Temple, depict three stories of eminent monks' pilgrimages in Chinese history.

The two figures on the left are the Indian monks Matanga and Dharmaratna (first century CE), who brought Buddhist sutras to China on white horses. The central carvings feature Zhu Shihang 朱士行 (203–282), the first Chinese monk to journey to the Western Regions in search of Buddhism teachings. The figure on the right represents Tripitaka portrayed as a compassionate, modest, and devout monk. Photographs by Wang Yixian.

bas-reliefs started to portray the simian disciple and guardian who accompanies the monk Xuanzang on his journey to India. The earliest existing grotto bas-reliefs that feature Tripitaka and Monkey paying tributes to the water-moon Avalokitesvara Guanyin are located in Cave 2 of the Zhongshan grottos in the Yan'an region of Shaanxi province. These bas-reliefs can be dated to 1112 CE during the Northern Song (960–1127). Thirteen more bas-reliefs were produced quickly within approximately ten years in this same region (Wei and Zhang, 2019: 2–4).

About the same time, a "journey to the West" grotto bas-relief was carved more than 1,200 kilometers from Shaanxi in Sichuan's Luzhou. One century later, at least six beautiful murals were painted in the Yulin 榆林 caves, Thousand-Buddha caves 千佛洞, and Mount Manjusri grottos of Guazhou in the late Xi Xia dynasty (1038–1227) (Figures 13 and 14). Between 1237 and 1250, two bas-reliefs of a monkey guardian were carved on a pagoda of the Kaiyuan temple of Quanzhou – a port city in Fujian that is 3,400 kilometers from Guazhou – in 1237–1250 (Wei and Zhang, 2019: 2–4) (Figure 15).

Figure 13 Tripitaka, accompanied by Monkey, paying homage to Bodhisattva Samantabhadra (Yulin Cave 3). Courtesy of Dunhuang Academy.

Figure 14 A mural that depicts the water-moon Avalokitesvara Guanyin, visited by Tripitaka and Monkey, who appear in the lower-right corner of the painting (Yulin Cave 2). Courtesy of Dunhuang Academy.

The strongest evidence of the *Ramayana*'s transmission to China is the monkey guardian in the sculptural relief on a panel at the fourth floor of one of the two pagodas (called the East and West Pagodas 東西塔) built in 1237 in the Kaiyuan 開元 temple in Quanzhou. The monkey guardian shares with Monkey a number of similarities: They are both holding a weapon and wearing a tight-fillet and identical earrings; they both have long hair and an elongated mouth; they have similar ornaments on their forearm and upper arm; and they both possess the ability to leap swiftly.

In short, the *Ramayana* was spread from India to Southeast Asia and to China. Stories of Hanuman were known to the Tibetans, Mongolians, Tocharians, ethnic peoples in the southwestern region of China, and the Han Chinese. Fostering a robust transregional Buddhist network that encompassed various regions, the first wave of globalism that happened around 1000 CE further facilitated the spread of the *Ramayana* and stories of Hanuman. Since then, the monkey disciple started to appear by the side of the legendary monk Xuanzang on the murals and bas-reliefs created in that period.

Figure 15 Bas-relief of a monkey guardian carved on the pagodas of the Kaiyuan Temple in Quanzhou. Holding a large knife, the monkey guardian wears a circular headband, Buddhist prayer beads, a short jacket, and Arhat shoes. A rope is tied around his waist from which dangle a gourd and a sutra scroll. Photograph by Xu Huaji.

Chinese Reception of Buddhist Deities

The "journey to the West" stories serve as a literary repository of the Buddhist pantheon, weaving deities from diverse Buddhist traditions and historical periods. Initially foreign to the Chinese, this pantheon was gradually assimilated, becoming the vital "world-making power" at the core of the narrative corpus. Compassion, heroism, protection, wisdom, and emptiness function as some of the governing laws of this literary universe.

The first deity to mention is Vaisravana, the god of protection. Originated in the kingdom of Khotan, this Tantric god resides in the north of Mount Meru in the Buddhist cosmos. Often portrayed as holding a mouse that can spit out gold ingots, this deity of luck and wealth protects armies, states, and people. In *The Story of the Monk*, Vaisravana helps Tripitaka to cross a deep pit, extinguish a wildfire, and halt the flow of a river so that he could continue his journey (Wang, 2011: 217–218). Vaisravana became so popular in the Dunhuang region in the Tang and the Five Dynasties (907–979) that Emperor Xuanzong (685–762) of the Tang requested the Tantric monk Amoghavajra (705–774) to summon Vaisravana

Figure 16 Painting of Vaisravana, Guardian of the North, shown crossing the waters, floating on purple clouds. In one hand, a golden halberd; in the other, a purple cloud supporting a stupa with a seated Buddha inside. Flames come out of his shoulders. His retinue includes Sri Devi, his sister, holding a golden dish of flowers, the sage Vasu, and one of Vaisravana's sons. Garuda flies above.
Courtesy of the British Museum.

to protect the Tang army in a battle against the Western Bod, Tajik, and Sogdian forces (Zan, 1987: 11–12) (Figure 16). In later stories and films, however, Vaisravana became conflated with and Sinicized into the pagoda-holding Daoist deity Li Jing whose third son, Nezha, is a beloved protective deity in Chinese popular tales.[16]

---

[16] The latest and most popular adaptations of Ne Zha's story are the animation blockbuster films *Ne Zha: the Demon Boy Descends to Earth* (2019) and *Ne Zha 2: Demon Child Is Back* (2024).

A second interesting deity to mention is Hariti – fertility goddess, healer, and protector of children transmitted to East Asia and Southeast Asia from Gandharan India influenced by Greco-Buddhism. In *The Story of the Monk*, Tripitaka visits the country of Hariti where he sees many three-year-old children living without their parents and where Hariti bestows elaborate gifts on Tripitaka and his disciples. In *Journey Drama 24*, Hariti is a demoness and mother of the demon Red Child who snatches Tripitaka. The Buddha then contains Red Child under his alms bowl in an attempt to convert Hariti so as to save the monk. Both the plots are based upon the hagiography of Hariti who was a child-eating demoness before her conversion. To convert her, the Buddha captures her youngest son, Pingala, and covers him under his magic alms bowl. After days of searching for her son in vain and realizing the pain she has inflicted upon parents, the distressed mother repents in front of the Buddha and converts to Buddhism. Hariti's cult reached its zenith in China and Japan between the ninth and eleventh centuries (Murray, 1981–1982: 256). Her cult became secularized after the Song dynasty, as demonstrated by the anonymous Yuan dynasty painting *Hariti Raising the Alms Bowl* 鬼子母揭缽圖 (Li, 2008) (Figure 17). Yet her cult declined in Ming–Qing China, probably in part because Bodhisattva Avalokitesvara rose to a prominent status.

Bodhisattva Avalokitesvara is the most important Buddhist deity in the entire "journey to the West" stories. The appearance of Avalokitesvara Guanyin 觀音, the goddess of compassion, is related to the rise of Mahayana Buddhism that began in India around the beginning of the Common Era. Retaining her bodhisattva form, Guanyin refused to ascend to Buddhahood because she wanted to stay with the sentient beings in the realm of life to save them from suffering. A savior (portrayed as holding a flask in the left hand and a willow branch in the right), a successor to Amitabha, and a personal devotional deity, Guanyin

Figure 17 *Hariti Raising the Alms Bowl*, by an anonymous artist in the Yuan dynasty. In the painting, an elegant lady in a pink silk dress looks agonized as she tries to rescue her child from the Buddha's alms bowl. The surrounding audience sympathizes with her distress. Courtesy of the Palace Museum of China.

emerged as the most responsive and sympathetic deity, beloved by people across East Asia (Wong, 2007).[17] In Chinese iconographic images first created at the end of the sixth century, she possesses many forms (Figures 18–19). In the grottos and murals in Dunhuang that depict Xuanzang's tribute to Guanyin, she is presented as the Water-Moon Bodhisattva (Figure 14). In *The Story of the Monk*, Avalokitesvara appears with 1,000 arms and 1,000 eyes in her Tantric form. In *Journey to the West*, Guanyin sometimes takes on the form of the fish-basket Bodhisattva (see also Figure 28 in Section 4 in the Element).

Figure 18 Mural of Guanyin (Southern wall, Mogao Cave 57), early Tang dynasty. Dressed in white, the bodhisattva wears a jeweled gold crown adorned with a Buddha icon, along with an intricate necklace draping across her neck and chest and multiple bracelets encircling her wrists and arms. Courtesy of Dunhuang Academy.

---

[17] The gender transformation of Guanyin from male to female is a unique Chinese phenomenon (Yu, 2001: 1–27). Guanyin was never worshipped as a goddess in India, Tibet, Sri Lanka, or Southeast Asia. In the Tang and Song periods, Guanyin began to assume the characteristics of a female deity. By the Ming dynasty, the Chinese generally regarded Guanyin as a female bodhisattva.

Figure 19 White-Robe Guanyin, Yanxia Cave of Hangzhou, Five Dyansties. Dressed in a white robe with a veil covering her headdress – adorned with a Buddha icon – the bodhisattva steps on lotus blossoms, holds prayer beads, and crosses her hands in a gesture symbolizing the Buddhist concept of nonduality. Photograph by Yuanfei Wang.

A crucial reason that Avalokitesvara Guanyin is the most significant deity in the "journey to the West" stories is because of her close association with the *Heart Sutra* that is at the core of Xuanzang's legendary pilgrimage. The *Heart Sutra*, as we know it today, begins with Guanyin's name:

觀自在菩薩	The noble Avalokitesvara Bodhisattva,
行深波若不羅密多時	while practicing the deep practice of Prajaparamita,
照見五蘊皆空	looked upon the Five Skandhas
度一切苦厄	and saw they were empty of self-existence. (Red Pine, 2004: 1)

This Chinese version of the *Heart Sutra* was actually composed by Xuanzang himself, who claimed that he found the original Sanskrit text of the *Heart Sutra* in India and then meticulously translated it into Chinese. Xuanzang's version of the *Heart Sutra* from the seventh century has been the standard translation throughout East Asia.

Because of the intimate tie between Xuanzang and the *Heart Sutra*, an all-powerful sacred text, historical and fictional accounts have attempted to unravel the mystery of Xuanzang's access to the supreme sacred scripture. The *Biography of the Tripitaka Dharma Master of the Great Compassionate Grace Temple of the Great Tang Dynasty* by Huili (b. 614) and Yan Zong relates an account of a sick old man that appeared in front of Xuanzang to give him the *Heart Sutra* as an aid in overcoming the difficulties of crossing the 800-tricent Gobi Desert (*Mohe yanqi*) right before his embarkment (Mair, 2002).[18]

> Beyond this place was the Mo-he-yen Desert, which stretched more than eight hundred tricents. This was what the ancients called the Sand River, where there was no bird flying above, nor any beast roaming below; neither was there any water or grass. Now the Master had only his lonely shadow traveling with him, and all he could do was repeat the name of Avalokitesvara Bodhisattva and recite the *Prajnaparamita-Hridaya Sutra*.
>
> Formerly, when the Master was in the region of Shu, he once saw a sick man suffering from a foul skin ulcer and dressed in filthy rags. With a feeling of pity, he took the man to the monastery and gave him money to purchase clothes and food. Out of gratitude, the sick man taught the Master this sutra, which he often recited. When he reached the Sand River, he met various evil spirts with strange appearances that surrounded him and refused to be dispelled completely, although he repeated the name of Avalokitesvara Bodhisattva. But as soon as he uttered this sutra, all of them disappeared at the sound of his voice. Truly, it was by depending upon this sutra that he was saved from many a peril. (Li, 1995b: 26–27)

The *Heart Sutra* was popular in Chan Buddhism, which values the spontaneous mind and sudden enlightenment without the aid of written texts. In *Journey to the West*, it is Crow's Nest Chan Master 烏巢禪師 living on a mountain who transmits the *Heart Sutra* to Tripitaka. Interestingly, in this novel, Tripitaka seems dimwitted. It is Monkey who keeps advising Tripitaka to recite the *Heart Sutra* whenever the monk feels anxious in the face of danger. In chapter 85, Monkey reminds Tripitaka of the four lines of the *gatha* from the *Heart Sutra*:

> Seek not afar for Buddha on Spirit Mount;
> Mount Spirit lives only inside your mind.
> There's in each man a Spirit Mount stupa;
> Beneath this stupa you must be refined.
>
> (Yu, 2012: vol. 4, 145)

---

[18] A tricent is one-third of a mile.

Chan Buddhism greatly influenced the "journey to the West" stories. It is generally believed that the first master of Chan Buddhism, Damo, was Bodhidharma from a Brahmin lineage in South India. In the Northern Wei period (386–534), he sailed on the South China Sea to arrive in Guangzhou and later journeyed northward to the heartland of China to teach Chan Buddhism (Figure 20). His main thesis is the "seal of the mind" (*xinyin* 心印), or truth, can be understood and realized directly through mind without the help of any written words, such as reading and reciting sutras (Mu'an, 1154: 185). As soon as he reaches Middle India, in *Journey Drama 24*, Tripitaka debates with an elderly Indian woman on what the "seal of the mind" is. Later, Anathapindada regards Tripitaka as a true bearer of the seal of the mind.

Figure 20 A Ming dynasty porcelain figurine of Damo, the Chan Master (Provincial Museum of Guangdong).

Legend has it that a farmer once encountered Damo on the road, holding one of his straw sandals. When asked where he was going, the master replied that he was heading to the Western Heaven. Later, the man realized that the master had passed away and attained nirvana. Photograph by Yuanfei Wang.

The "seal of the mind" emphasizes verbal conversations and a detached mind. As a result, riddle-like conversations and the concept of nonduality (bu'er 不二) are the crucial elements in Chan Buddhism. In a Chan conversation, the master's answers should be quick, short, witty, and riddle-like. Chan disciples seek enlightenment precisely through wrestling with these verbal puzzles (Cunningham, 2011: 15). As for the concept of nonduality, the conversation on the Buddha's nature between the sixth Chan Patriarch Huineng 惠能 (638–713) of the Southern Sect of Chan Buddhism and his teacher, Hongren 弘忍 (601–675), as recounted in *The Platform Sutra* 六祖壇經, reveals that the Buddha's nature is nonduality – neither good nor bad, neither constant nor inconstant.[19]

Nonduality governs the theme of the Yuan play *The Wild Ape* which delivers the message that the duality of animals and humans as ordinary folks assume prevents them from seeing the Buddha's nature of nonduality. It tells how an ape can be enlightened after having listened to a Chan master's teaching of the Buddhist scriptures for 1,000 years. Even though the ape possesses an animal's form (inferior to human form), he can reach enlightenment by listening to the teaching of the master, conversing with the master, and meditating on Buddhist scriptures.

> This junior scholar is not a human. I am an old ape who has obtained the Dao in the mountain. Because I was not enlightened by a sacred monk or a *luohan* (arhat; saint), I could not transcend samsara. Earlier, I had transformed into a Confucian woodcutter who listened to the instruction of the master. By then, I had already recognized half of the truth of Buddhism. Later, I entered the meditation hall of the master in my simian form, and he taught me the Buddhist canon and gave me his *kasaya* (robe). I was fortunate that the teacher did not discriminate against me. Today at your seat, master, I listened again to a few true words from you, which have enlightened the heart of this beast. I have indeed completely realized the truth! (Zhao, 1958: 17)

This tale of an enlightened ape can be traced back to the life story of Upagupta (c. third century BCE), the fourth Patriarch of Chan Buddhism as recounted in the *Sutra of the Wise and the Foolish* and given the fullest treatment in the *Mulasarvastivada Vinaya* (Strong, 1992: 44–56). In the *Sutra of the Wise and the Foolish*, Upagupta relates that in his previous life he was a monkey. He wandered around and came across 500 *pratyekabuddhas*.[20] He offered them leaves, flowers, and fruits and admired and imitated their meditating posture by sitting down and crossing his legs. After the nirvana of the *pratyekabuddhas*, the monkey encountered 500 Brahmanical ascetics who were

---

[19] Zongbao 宗寶, ed., *The Platform Sutra* 六祖壇經. CBETA Chinese Electronic Tripitaka Collection CBETA 佛教電子佛典集成. https://cbetaonline.dila.edu.tw/zh/.

[20] A *pratyekabuddha* is an individual who independently achieves liberation.

engaged in painful ascetic practices. Some of them held their legs high while others were doing the penance of fire. The monkey then went forward to lower their legs and extinguish the fire and then sat down and crossed his legs. Realizing that the monkey was showing them the meditating posture, they immediately mimicked his posture and practiced meditation like the monkey. Upagupta's karmic past shows that dharma was in his nature. Even when he was still a monkey, he helped people to reach enlightenment.

Magical Combat and Karmic Retribution

Buddhism has influenced the narrative structure of *Journey to the West*. Two salient aspects should be mentioned: One is the magical battles between the demons and deities in their delusory forms, and the other is the law of karmic retribution that decides the fates of the characters. First, a major literary representation of the fantastic adventures in *Journey to the West* is the trope of magical combat. The archetype for this comes from the transformation texts and Buddhist stories as exemplified by the *Transformation on the Subduing of Demons*. Consider the similarity between the following two depictions. The first paragraph, excerpted from the *Transformation on the Subduing of Demons*, depicts the magical transformations of Sariputra and his non-Buddhist opponent Raudraksa:

> Suddenly, Raudraksa conjured up a water-buffalo in the midst of the assembly. His buffalo had sparkling horns which startled the heavens. Its four hoofs were like Damascus swords. A hanging dewlap trailed on the ground. Its twin pupils were as bright as the sun and the moon. It bellowed once – thunder rumbled and lightning crackled. The spectators gasped in amazement, and everyone said that the heretics had taken the lead.
>
> Although Sariputra saw this buffalo, his expression remained unchanged. Suddenly, he conjured up a lion whose ferocity was not to be challenged. His lion had
>
>> A mouth like a mountain gorge,
>> A body similar to a snow-covered mountain,
>> Eyes comparable to shooting stars,
>> And teeth like cold steel.
>> With a rousing roar,
>> It leaped right into the middle of the arena.
>> When the water-buffalo saw the lion,
>> It lost pluck and knelt on the ground.
>
> Then the lion
>
>> First seized the buffalo's nape,
>> Next snapped its spinal column;

> Before the lion was able to devour it,
> The buffalo's body broke into pieces.
> The Potentate gasped with surprise,
> The officials and commoners were taken aback.
>
> (Mair, 1983: 76)

The following description of the magical battles between Erlang and Monkey is taken from *Journey to the West*:

> Erlang at once discovered that the Great Sage had changed into a small sparrow perched on a tree. He changed out of his magic form and took off his pellet bow. With a shake of his body, he changed into a sparrow hawk with outstretched wings, ready to attack its prey. When the Great Sage saw this, he darted up with a flutter of his wings; changing himself into a cormorant, he headed straight for the open sky. When Erlang saw this, he quickly shook his feathers and changed into a huge ocean crane, which could penetrate the clouds to strike with its bill. The Great Sage therefore lowered his direction, changed into a small fish, and dove into a stream with a splash. Erlang rushed to the edge of the water but could see no trace of him. He thought to himself, "This simian must have gone into the water and changed himself into a fish, a shrimp, or the like. I'll change again to catch him." He duly changed into a fish hawk and skimmed downstream over the waves. For a while, the fish into which the Great Sage had changed was swimming along with the current. Suddenly he saw a bird that looked like a green kite though its feathers were not entirely green, like an egret though it had small feathers, and like an old crane though its feet were not red. "That must be the transformed Erlang waiting for me," he thought to himself. He swiftly turned around and swam away after releasing a few bubbles. When Erlang saw this, he said, "The fish that released the bubbles looks like a carp though its tail is not red, like a perch though there are no patterns on its scales, like a snake fish though there are no stars on its head, like a bream though its gills have no bristles. Why does it move away the moment it sees me? It must be the transformed monkey himself!" (Yu, 2012: vol. 1, 183)

These two paragraphs both demonstrate the notion of *nirmana* ("metamorphosis") central to Mahayana Buddhism which means magical creation produced through transformation. The illusory forms created through metamorphosis are meant for Buddhists to convince the nonbelievers of the power of the dharma. In *Journey to the West*, as well as in many other late imperial works of Chinese fiction, metamorphosis becomes a general trope for any magical combat that is not necessarily Buddhist.

Second, the theme of karmic retribution is common in *Journey to the West*, as well as in other late imperial popular literature (Bantly, 1989; Kao, 1989; Mair, 1983: 9; Wang, 2024). For instance, Tripitaka is the reincarnation of a disciple of the Buddha – Master Golden Cicada. Pigsy's previous incarnation was

Marshal Heavenly Mugwort before he was banished from Heaven and went through the cycle of reincarnation. Major traditional novels such as *Water Margin*, *Plum in the Golden Vase*, and *Dream of the Red Chamber* all have karmic retribution as their narrative thread.

Concluding Remarks

The legendary monk Xuanzang's travels to India have inspired a vast literary and artistic legacy, sparking countless stories, artworks, films, and performances in China from medieval times to the present day. This global fascination with reimagining and retelling the heroic monk's epic journey shows no sign of fading. Yet few realize that behind the "global story" of the "journey to the West" tales lies another ancient "global story" of the *Ramayana*. It traveled across borders, moving from India to Southeast Asia and eventually into the heartland of China. Like the "journey to the West" stories, the *Ramayana* was disseminated gradually and fragmentarily through individual episodes, translation, paraphrasing, summary, adaptation, and diverse art forms like literature, theater, oral storytelling, paintings, murals, and sculpture. It is no exaggeration to say that the *Ramayana* played an indispensable role in the shaping of the beloved Monkey in Chinese literature.

Buddhist literary diffusion shaped the imaginative world of the "journey to the West" narratives and, by extension, Chinese literature itself. The stories serve as a reservoir of Buddhist thoughts and schools, which then turn into the world-making force of the corpus. These stories construct a brave new world that champions compassion, heroism, protection, enlightenment, and emptiness. Integrated into the mechanism of karmic retribution, these values intertwine with the fantastical adventures of magic battles. Transcending geographical, national, and cultural divides, this literary world speaks not just to humanity but to all sentient beings: animals, plants, and spirits alike, weaving a cosmic unity that stretches from the Middle Ages to the digital age.

PART II SEA AND STORY

Introduction to Part II

Before the eighth century, China's court largely neglected the oceanic space and southern coasts. No archaeological or textual evidence shows that maritime ships were made in China until the twelfth century (Sen, 2017: 536, 539). The famous Belitung shipwreck which carried the single biggest collection of Tang dynasty Changsha ceramics and gold and silver objects found outside of China was an Arabian dhow that sank around 830 CE on its return voyage from China and was excavated near the coast of Belitung Island, Indonesia. This shipwreck already indicates the existence of a thriving maritime trade between the Arab world and China in the ninth century (Figure 21).

In the twelfth century, the Song court started to encourage maritime commerce due to the Chanyuan treaty signed with the Khitan Liao that pushed the Chinese to seek expansion in the southern seas (Hansen, 2020: 25). Thus, the Song-Yuan-Ming period witnessed a significant expansion of maritime routes connecting China with India and Southeast Asia. Traders, religious practitioners, diplomats, officials, soldiers, and adventurers were able to sail in these global maritime networks that were not previously available in the first millennium (Sen, 2006). In the Ming dynasty, Zheng He's seven voyages largely expanded Ming China's maritime networks in the Indian Ocean (Wade, 2004) (Figure 22).

During this time period, many important geographical accounts and travelogues were written, published, and circulated simply because their authors were able to travel on the sea and visit coastal places from one port to another, curious about the exotic and the unfamiliar. For instance, Zhu Yu 朱彧, collected his observations made between the 1070s and 1080s during his visits to the foreign quarters in Guangzhou and authored *Matters Worth Discussing from Pingzhou* (*Pingzhou ketan* 萍洲可談, 1119). Zhou Qufei's 周去非 (1135–1189) *Representative Answers from the Region beyond the Mountains* 嶺外代答 (1178) collected

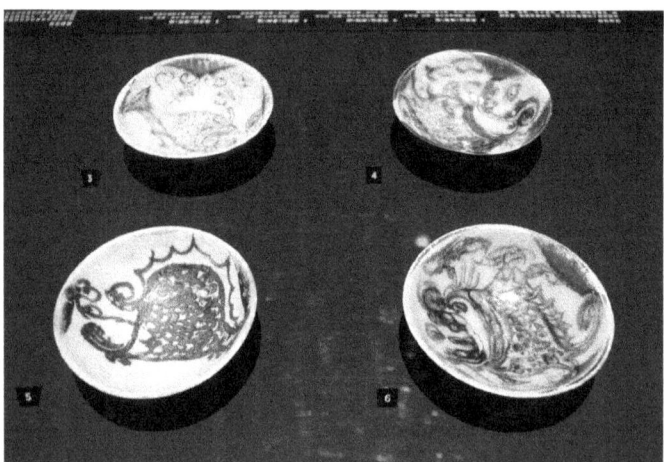

Figure 21 Ceramic bowls from the Tang shipwreck at Belitung (The Asian Civilisations Museum, Singapore). These bowls, painted with intricate fish patterns, are among the 50,000 hand-painted bowls discovered in the shipwreck. The bowls were produced in Changsha, Hunan province, around the 830s CE. Wikipedia Commons.

Figure 22 A model of Zheng He's treasure fleets (Hong Kong Maritime Museum). Photograph by Yuanfei Wang.

information gathered in Guangxi in 1170s. Liu Xun's 劉恂 *Lingbiao luyi* 嶺表錄異 is based upon the northerner's tenure as an official in Guangzhou. Wang Dayuan 汪大淵 (1311–1350) composed *A Brief Record of Barbarian Islands* 島夷志略 after many years of maritime voyages. Zhao Rukuo 赵汝适 (1170–1230) wrote *Zhufan zhi* 諸蕃志 (1225) based upon his conversations and interviews with foreign maritime merchants in Quanzhou where he served as an official of the shipping bureau. Admiral Zheng He's 鄭和 Muslim translator and recorder Ma Huan 馬歡 accompanied the commander to visit kingdoms in Southeast Asia, the Middle East, and Eastern Africa across the Indian Ocean. His travelogue *Overall Survey of the Ocean's Shores* 瀛涯勝覽 (1451) is hence based upon firsthand empirical experience and personal observations.

Part II, "Sea and Story," will explore two modes of literary diffusion facilitated by the ship. Section 4 charts the remarkable seafaring journeys of early Cinderella stories as they sailed across cultures. The tale absorbed local flavor and morphed into a nativized shape as it reached a new shore. Simplicity and adaptability are Cinderella's magic – the quality that allows the tale to slip effortlessly between languages and cultures while always striking at the universal core of the human psyche.

Section 5 will explore two examples of Ming dynasty drama and fiction from Admiral Zheng He's seven voyages on the Indian Ocean. This section showcases "indirect literary diffusion" that manifests how Zheng He's global journeys and the new knowledge of the world brought back to China are represented in literature. That world knowledge in literature is secondhand, since the authors never traveled abroad and just compiled the geographical knowledge from the travelogues and information available to them through commercial printing, hearsay, and popular culture.

In all, Part II of this Element features the kind of literary diffusion that is facilitated by ships. Premodern ships were the vehicle of global transmission par excellence, since they were able to travel long distances, covering most of the globe – the saltwater zone – and reaching many countries in a relatively short period of time, not to mention that the carrying capacity of ships is enormous compared with any form of land travel.

4 Maritime Circulation of the Cinderella Story

The Cinderella story is one of the world's best-loved and most widely known fairy tales. Most children around the globe have probably heard of the miserable "ash maiden" who marries a prince after she rushes to get back home and loses her glass slipper. There are more than 2,000 versions of the Cinderella story throughout the world, with all sorts of variants that contain a host of different elements and episodes. One of the world's earliest versions of the Cinderella story comes from the Chinese tale of a girl named Yexian 葉限 (hereafter, the Yexian story) that can be found in the Tang dynasty collection of exotica, *Miscellaneous Morsels from Youyang* (*Youyang zazu* 酉陽雜俎) by Duan Chengshi 段成式 (803–863) and published in the ninth century. This story, although included in a Chinese language anthology, is based upon an oral rendition by a person of Zhuang ethnicity – a non-Sinitic people living in China's far southern reaches (nowadays Nanning of the Guangxi Zhuang Autonomous Region). Certain questions arise from this: Is this the origin of the Cinderella story? If the original story was from elsewhere, how did it reach Guangxi in ninth-century Tang China?

It is impossible to determine the very first version, but early folklorists attempted to trace the development of the tale globally. Anna Birgitta Rooth (1951), for instance, argued that the story originated in the East, developed in the Near East, and then spread across all of Europe. Naitong Ding (1974) proposes that the Cinderella story's ancient tradition probably started in a small Vietnamese village between Hanoi and Haiphong. The story spread to

Guangdong and Guangxi and then westward to Yunnan and Tibet (Ding, 1974: 32) before traveling to Europe. Fay Beauchamp (2010) further emphasizes the originality of the Zhuang version, the Yexian story, arguing that this Cinderella story was first told among the Zhuang people at the crossroads of China and Vietnam.

We surmise, however, that the Cinderella story ultimately originated in western Eurasia and underwent significant developments in South Asia before finding its way to Southeast Asia and then circulated among the Zhuang people in Guangxi. From there, it was relayed to central China (Mair, 2005: 364). Since the early Cinderella stories mainly spread along southern Eurasian coasts, we believe that the Cinderella story was transmitted primarily by sea. In the following, we will trace Cinderella's seaborn journeys across continents. This highly mobile story continuously absorbed local favor and reinvented itself as it reached a new shore.

The Lost Slipper, the Fish, and the Stepmother: An Indian Adaptation

The earliest Cinderella story is derived from "Rhodopis" related by the Greek geographer Strabo (c. 64 BCE–24 CE) in the early first century CE. According to the story, when the beautiful courtesan Rhodopis was bathing at Naucratis, an eagle perching nearby snatched one of her sandals and flew away. It then dropped the sandal in the lap of the Egyptian king in Memphis. Enthralled by the beauty of the sandal, the king searched for its fair owner and then married her (Smith, 1867: 268). This motif of an eagle and a sandal also appears in a Greek constellation myth recorded by the Latin author Gaius Julius Hyginus (64 BCE–17 CE) who states that Jupiter sent an eagle to snatch Venus's sandal while she was bathing. Jupiter then gave it to Mercury in Amythaonia of Egypt after Venus had rejected Mercury (Ben-Amos, 2010: 439).

In the first century CE, the lost slipper story traveled from southern Greece to India. By then, Greece already had extensive cultural contact with India. In the third century BCE, Alexander the Great (356–323 BCE) conquered the Achaemenid Persian empire and expanded his empire to northwestern India, along the lowest areas of the Indus River. In the aftermath of this conquest, Demetrius I Anicetus (r. c. 200–161 BCE) ruled the region from Bactria to northwestern India. Macedon absorbed Gandhara, resulting in a distinctive syncretic Gandhara-style culture exemplified by Greco-Buddhism that flourished between the fourth century BCE and the fifth century CE. *The Periplus of the Erythraean Sea*, an eyewitness account of ancient maritime voyages to

Africa and India via the Red Sea written around the middle of the first century CE in *koinè* Greek by an unknown trader or shipowner living in Roman Egypt, records a popular route along which the Greek lost slipper story could have spread to India. The voyager sailed from the ports of Myos Hormos and Berenice Troglodytica on the western edge of Egypt, along the Red Sea, then eastward to Avalites, Malao, passing Barbaroi, the coast of Azania, Arabia, the Erythraean Sea, the Persian Gulf, and then to the west coast of India (Casson, 2012: 51–91) (see Figure A4 in the Appendix and the online resources).

While the Greek story concerns solely how a lost slipper leads to a beautiful girl's ascendance in social status from slave to royalty, Hinduism and Buddhism transformed the Greek lost slipper story profoundly. In Indian versions, the girl is rewarded not because she is beautiful but because she is compassionate. She saves a fish, and this changes everything. Although the Indian versions of the Cinderella story have been lost, the earliest Chinese version, the Yexian story, preserves the Buddhist and Hindu elements that were formed in India.

The Yexian story goes like this. A tribal leader surnamed Wu whom the aborigines called "Cave Wu" near present-day Nanning in Guangxi Province has two wives, one of whom dies, leaving him a daughter named Yexian. He adores this girl who is skilled at gathering gold by sifting for it in water. However, he soon dies as well. Thereafter, his second wife, Yexian's stepmother, constantly mistreats her, forcing her to cut wood in the dangerous mountains and to get water from the deep lakes and rivers. One day Yexian catches a golden fish from a river. She secretly raises the fish in a basin, but soon the fish grows so big that no household vessel can contain it. She then puts it in a pond behind her house, feeding it daily with all her leftover food. The fish trusts only Yexian and surfaces only when it sees her reflection from under the water. One day, clad in Yexian's clothes, the stepmother comes to the pond and calls the fish's name. Deceived by her reflection, the fish appears. The stepmother captures and then cooks and eats the fish. When Yexian returns and discovers this, a deity in coarse clothes and unkempt hair appears and tells her to bring the fish bones home and hide them. If she prays to the fish bones, her wishes will come true. One day, the stepmother and her daughter go to a festival dressed in their finest. She orders Yexian to stay home to watch their fruit trees. Yexian then prays to the fish bones in the hope that she can also go to the festival. Her wish comes true! In kingfisher-blue clothes and golden shoes, she enjoys her time at the festival until her stepmother sees her. Afraid that her stepmother may have recognized her, Yexian hurries home, accidentally leaving one gold shoe behind. A man finds the shoe and trades it with the king of Tuohan who rules over a score of maritime islands. As light as a feather, the shoe mesmerizes the Tuohan ruler and he orders all the women on his islands to try it on. As expected, no one's foot fits the shoe until Yexian is found. The Tuohan king then marries her and takes her and her fish bones to his island. The stepmother and her daughter are stoned to death. Their tomb is called the "Tomb of Regret." The king becomes greedy, constantly praying for treasures, so after one year, the fish bones stop responding. He then buries the bones by the shore until one day the waves wash them away (Mair, 2005: 363–367).

Although the Yexian story is a Chinese tale, many of the Hindu-Buddhist elements in it were formed earlier, at the same time that the Greek lost slipper story was nativized in India. Three major events demonstrate this view: (1) a girl saves a small golden fish that grows into a big fish; (2) the bones of the fish have wish-fulfilling powers that lead to the girl becoming the first wife of a powerful king; and (3) because the girl has a horrible stepmother, she lives in wretched conditions until she is saved by an animal and identified by her lost shoe that eventually connects her to royalty.

The first major event in the story is that the girl saves a small fish that keeps growing until it is a giant fish that she raises in the pond in her backyard. Beauchamp (2010: 466) rightly points out that the Hindu story of Manu from the *Satapatha Bhramana* (*Brahmana of One Hundred Paths*) is the origin of this giant fish motif:

> In the morning they brought to Manu water for washing, just as now also they (are wont to) bring (water) for washing the hands. When he was washing himself, a fish came into his hands. It spake to him the word, "Rear me, I will save thee!" "Wherefrom wilt thou save me?" "A flood will carry away all these creatures: from that I will save thee!" "How am I to rear thee?" It said, "As long as we are small, there is great destruction for us: fish devours fish. Thou wilt first keep me in a jar. When I outgrow that, thou wilt dig a pit and keep me in it. When I outgrow that, thou wilt take me down to the sea, for then I shall be beyond destruction." It soon became a *ghasha* (a large fish); for that grows largest (of all fish).... Thereupon it said, "In such and such a year that flood will come. Thou shalt then attend to me (i.e. to my advice) by preparing a ship; and when the flood has risen thou shalt enter into the ship, and I will save thee from it." After he had reared it in this way, he took it down to the sea. (Brahmana, 1882: 216–217; Beauchamp, 2010: 466)

The three-step process – the fish moving gradually from a water jar to a pond and then to the sea – echoes the multiple changes of water containers in the Yexian story: "She put it in a bowl of water and raised it. Day by day it grew, causing her to change the bowl several times. It grew so big that no bowl could hold it; consequently she threw it into the pond out back" (Mair, Steinhardt, and Goldin, 2005: 364) (Figure 23).

Figure 23 Stephenie Law's painting titled *With Pure Heart* portraying the girl Yexian and the golden fish she saved. Courtesy of Stephenie Law.

In Mahayana Buddhism there is a variant of the idea that a giant fish can save people in times of natural disaster. In volume seven of the *Sutra of the Wise and the Foolish*, the Buddha tells Ananda that in one of his previous lives, he transformed into a giant fish to rescue people. In that life, he was the king of Jambudvipa, a continent in ancient Indian cosmogony. One day, a huge ball of fire suddenly appeared in the sky that would cause twelve years of drought in the kingdom. When crops did not grow, more and more commoners died of hunger. To save his people from dying, the king vowed to turn into a giant fish. Indeed, woodcutters working by the sea found a giant fish who asked them to eat its flesh to survive. Eventually, everyone in the country fed on the fish meat for twelve years until the drought was over (Sha, 2021: 133). This story of how the king volunteered to turn into a fish to be eaten by his starving people is a Buddhist tale. Behind the tale is the key concept in Mahayana Buddhism – compassion. Similarly, the Yexian story is a Buddhist tale. The Buddhist concept of karma was the basis for the belief that the terrible stepmother who devoured the fish deserved to be punished.

The second significant event that occurs is that the fish bones have a magic power that rewards the girl for her compassion by letting her rise in social status to become a queen. This resonates with a story in the *Golden Light Sutra* (*Suvarnaprabhasa Sutra*), a Mahayana Buddhist scripture that relates how an elderly man named the Old Man of Flowing Water rescued 10,000 fish from a lake that was drying up. The compassionate man borrowed twenty elephants from the king and loaded them with innumerable gallons of water contained in wineskins to refill the lake. He then used all his food to feed the fish, thus saving the 10,000 fish. Many years later, after the creatures had passed away, their souls ascended to heaven where they became 10,000 princes. To thank the old man, one day they appeared in the sky and showered him with jewels, pearls, and flowers.

The *Golden Light Sutra* is one of the earliest Mahayana sutras to flourish at the beginning of the Common Era. The old man's rescue of fish resonates with the profound merit of Yexian's rescuing the fish, pointing to Mahayana Buddhism's influence in the Yexian story. The Greek story about a beautiful girl's lost slipper, thus transformed. The Indo-Scythian monk Lokaksema (active 147–189 CE) from the kingdom of Gandhara is known for introducing Mahayana Buddhism to China by translating many Mahayana sutras including the *Astasahasrika Prajnaparamita Sutra*. However, in addition to the translated scriptures, sermons, and semireligious stories, lay Buddhist tales were already circulating in South Asia, Central Asia, and China in the form of literature. That is, some secular folktales such as the early Cinderella story may have been influenced by Mahayana Buddhism to the extent that the core concept of compassion constituted the frame of this popular tale.

Third, the girl who is at the center of the story has a terrible stepmother who makes her live in abysmal conditions until she is saved by an animal and identified by her shoe, whose loss eventually leads to her marrying the king. This resonates with the Dasaratha-Jataka version of Sita's story that is based upon the *Ramayana* (Beauchamp, 2010: 468–469). Although Fay Beauchamp argues that the *Ramayana* spread across Southeast Asia from the sixth to the eighth century, during which time it influenced the Yexian story, it is possible that an early version of the Cinderella story had already appeared in India through the influence of the *Ramayana* in its various forms such as Jataka tales. These tales are generally short and easy to read; they relate the Buddha's experiences in his former lives before he reached nirvana. Many Jataka tales are collected in the *Sutra of the Wise and the Foolish* that became very popular in Dunhuang and, to some extent, across central China, from the fifth century on.

The *Ramayana* relates that the King of Ayodhya, Dasaratha, has two wives, Kausalya and Kaikeyi, who vie to have their own sons, Rama and Bharata, designated the future king. The rivalry results in Rama's undergoing fourteen years of exile with his wife Sita. Sita is abducted during the exile and her golden anklet is dropped. Later, refusing Bharata's request to return to the palace to ascend the throne after the death of their father, Rama gives his slipper to his brother as a symbol of his sovereignty. Then Hanuman, a monkey with superpowers, comes to the rescue of Rama and Sita (Beauchamp, 2010: 468). In the Dasaratha-Jataka, Sita and Rama have a "happily-ever-after" ending, while in Valmiki's *Ramayana*, Rama repeatedly suspects Sita's loyalty, and Sita chooses death after demonstrating her faithfulness to Rama.

The earliest Egyptian version of the beautiful courtesan Rhodopis's missing sandal still holds sway in this early Indian version of the Cinderella story. Nonetheless, the Hindu *Ramayana* narrative creeps in to complicate the Greek tale. The new storyline is that the father has two wives. The child protagonist has to compete with a sibling in order to gain the favor of the father. When the father dies, the protagonist is cast into a miserable situation until an animal with supernatural powers comes to the rescue. After a journey of struggle, the protagonist is identified as the authentic sovereign through his shoe, leading to a happy ending.

Tuohan, Jewels, and Tides: A Thai Adaptation

Departing from India, the Cinderella story again set sail to accompany its storytellers – sailors, traders, and monks – to distant shores. The monsoon winds across the Bay of Bengal took the travelers from India to Southeast Asia. They stopped by the "roof" of the Bay of Bengal – today Bengal, Bangladesh, and Burma – before arriving at the northwestern shore of the Gulf of Siam (Tagliacozzo, 2022: 149). There, they discovered a thriving kingdom with a long coastline, ruling more than twenty maritime islands. As these voyagers interacted and intermarried with the local people and settled in this promising land, the Cinderella story thrived again, bolstered by Hinduism and Mahayana Buddhism.

Local Thai people were captivated by the story of a kind girl who saved a small fish that led to her social ascendance. They loved this story so much that they altered the storyline by including their own country, Tuohan. In this new version, the king is no longer Egyptian or Indian, but from Tuohan. Scholars have speculated about the various possible locations of Tuohan. For instance, the modern-day dictionary *The Collected Name Exegesis of Ancient Southern Sea* 古代南海地名匯釋 identifies the kingdom of Tuohan, also known as Tuohuan, as in the southeast of Myanmar – Tavoy (today Dawei) – or as Rangoon in Siam (Chen, Xie, and Lu, 1986: 464). R. D. Jameson (1982: 77–78) thinks that Tuohan was on Sumatra. Others believe it was a subordinate kingdom of Srivijiaya (Wang, 2006: 14), yet some dispute this view (Zhou, 2018).

We believe that the country of Tuohan was a maritime kingdom affiliated with Dvaravati (Ch. Duoheluo 墮和羅), an ancient kingdom in Thailand located on the lower reaches of the Chao Phraya River from the sixth to the tenth century. This legendary land is the oldest recognized kingdom in Thailand. Two silver medals found in Nakhon Pathom province in 1943 bear Sanskrit inscriptions that read "*sridvaravatisvarapunya*" ("the meritorious act of the king of Dvaravati"; Brown, 1996: xxii) and corroborate scholars' conjecture that the kingdom of Dvaravati existed in the region. Its ruins, now listed as a UNESCO site, are in present-day Si Thep, the southernmost district of Phetchabun province in central Thailand, 230 kilometers from Bangkok. The earliest record of the country comes from the travel accounts of the eminent Chinese Buddhist monk Xuanzang:

> Northeast of that [the country of Samatata in Bengal] in the valley beside the great sea is the country of Shili Chadaluo 室利差呾羅國 (Sri Ksetra; probably the Pyu capital, near present-day Pyay); further to the southeast of the great sea is the country of Kamalanka 迦摩浪迦國 (possibly Langkasuka); further to the east is the country of Dvarapati; and even further to the east is the country of Isanapura (Sambor Prei Kuk); to the east beyond that is the country of Mahacampa, which in our country is known as Linyi (Champa), and farther to the southeast is the country of Yamanadvipa 閻摩那洲國 (possible locations: Java, Sumatra, or Indochina). (Wade, 2014: 27)

The New History of the Tang Dynasty states:

> Duoheluo is also named Duheluo. To the south is the country of Pan Pan 盤盤, and to the north is the country of Jialuoshefu 迦羅舍弗. Its western border is adjacent to the sea. Its eastern neighbor is Cambodia. Embarking from Guangzhou and traveling for five months, one can reach the country. The country produces beautiful rhinoceros horns which are known as Dvaravati horns. It has two vassal countries: Tambralinga 曇陵 and Tuohuan 陀洹. (Ouyang, 1975: 6303)

Dvaravati was a major country in Southeast Asia that was strongly influenced by India. The *Ramayana*, and to some extent, the *Mahabharata*, impacted the arts, religions, and rulers of Dvaravati from the fourth to eighth centuries (Beauchamp, 2010: 468). Two stone images of Krishna lifting up Mount Govardhana and two stone images of Surya (the sun god) that date to the sixth to eighth century CE were excavated from Si Thep (Srisuchat, 2005: 109).

The Cinderella story underwent an interesting transformation again in the Dvaravati kingdom and the islands that it governed. Three of the events in the story are listed as proof: (1) the Tuohan king uses the treasures buried together with the fish bones to reward his soldiers; (2) the sea tides wash away the fish bones and the treasures that are buried near the sea; and (3) the name of Dvaravati is referenced in the Hindu epic the *Mahabharata*.

In the first event, the king of Tuohan rewards his soldiers with pearls buried with the fish bones at the seashore. The archetype of this plotline is from the *Lotus Sutra* that dates to the beginning of the Common Era. In that sutra, the powerful Wheel Turning King always wins battles against his neighboring kingdoms. With great delight, he honors his most capable military soldiers with precious pearls that he keeps carefully hidden in his tightly fixed hairdo. This parable illustrates the idea that the *Lotus Sutra* is an important text that brings enlightenment to its listeners. Therefore, a Buddhist monk would not easily teach it to a common audience, hence the metaphor of hiding the pearls in his hairdo (Sha, 2021: 211). The Dvaravati kingdom adopted the Buddhist symbol, the Wheel of the Law (*dharmachakra*) as its single most important symbol. The wheel elevated on a pillar was unique to the Mon territories of Thailand. According to the *Lotus Sutra*, the Wheel Turning King will rule the world when he gains possession of the golden turning wheel that will appear in the sky. Through its allusion to the Wheel Turning King, the Yexian story portrays the ruler of Tuohan as similar to the Wheel Turning King (Figure 24).

Figure 24 The Wheel of the Law (limestone) Dhammacakka (National Museum, Bangkok, Thailand). Wikipedia Commons.

Second, sea waves wash away the precious jewels. In the Buddhist cosmos, the ocean is the place where countless treasures are hidden, and only a person with compassion can obtain the gems from the sea. This cosmic view is manifested in a Buddhist story included in the *Sutra of the Wise and the Foolish* and the *Sutra of the Great Skillful Means of Repayment of Kindness*. The story is about a prince called the "friend of virtue" (*kalyanamitra*) and another prince called the "friend of greed" (*akalyana-mitrata*). Both hope to sail to the ocean to seek treasures. However, the greedy prince overloads his ship with treasures, leading to a shipwreck. The virtuous prince, on the other hand, overcomes a number of challenges and succeeds in reaching the dragon palace under the sea where he obtains the dragon king's *cintamani*, a large *mani* jewel that has the power to grant wishes. The message is that the worldly pursuit of money and status cannot compete with the spiritual pursuit of compassion and mercy, as this is the Buddhist path to truth. Not only does the dualism in the Yexian story as depicted by the kind-hearted girl and her greedy stepmother and sisters echo the same dichotomy as the Buddhist tale (the kind prince versus the greedy prince) but the fish's wish-fulfilling magic finds resonance in the *mani* pearl. Additionally, Buddhists believe that the pearl can be found in a legendary fish called the Makara – the vehicle of the river goddess Ganga, or the god of the ocean, Varuna.

Moreover, Daravati is a Sanskrit name, meaning "many gates" (Wade, 2014: 27). The name is directly referenced in the chapter "Mausala Parya" in the *Mahabharata* as a kingdom that is submerged by the sea.

> After all the people had set out, the ocean, that home of sharks and alligators, flooded Dwaraka, which still teemed with wealth of every kind, with its waters. Whatever portion of the ground was passed over, ocean immediately flooded over with his waters. Beholding this wonderful sight, the inhabitants of Dwaraka walked faster and faster, saying, "Wonderful is the course of fate!" (Roy, 1884–1894: 406)

By naming their kingdom Dvaravati, the early Thai people must have known of its portrayal in the Indian epic, with the seaborne reference in mind.[21] The underlying anxiety over the sea waves brushing away all the treasures on the island may be a reference to the *Mahabharata*.

Very likely, Tuohan was a thriving port that formed both diplomatic and economic ties with China and was an active participant in the maritime trade

---

[21] Although the *Mahabharata* was not as well-known as the *Ramayana* among the Thai ruling elite, they, nonetheless, were familiar with it. There was a prince by the name of Yudhisthira in Sukhothai-Phitsanulok area who broke away from Ayutthaya and allied with Chiang Mai. Yudhisthira was an important character in the *Mahabharata*. We thank Charnvit Kasetsiri for providing this information.

network connecting the South China Sea to the Indian Ocean. *The Old History of the Tang* records:

> The country of Tuohuan is located in the sea to the southwest of Lâm Ấp (an ancient kingdom in central Vietnam). Its northwestern border is adjacent to Dvaravati. It takes more than three months to reach Jiaozhi [corresponding to present-day north Vietnam] which is subordinate to Dvaravati. The king of Tuohuan is surnamed Chashili and his given name is Pomopona. Mulberry trees and silkworms cannot grow there. The people wear white clothes. By custom, the people all live in raised buildings which are called "stilt houses." In the eighteenth year of the Zhenguan reign era (644 CE) they sent emissaries to China. In the twenty-first year (647 CE) again, the king of Tuohan presented white parrots and camphor oil as tribute to China, requesting horses and copper bells in return. The emperor granted their wishes. (Liu, 1975: 5272)

The route that the embassies of Tuohuan took may also have been the route that merchants took to reach China. Since Tuohuan was located on a maritime island, the traders and diplomats went to China by ship. They passed by Vietnam then landed at the border between China and Vietnam, probably near the seaport of Haiphong, before they proceeded to travel to Nanning and then to their destinations – the heartland of China and the capital of Tang China, Chang'an, which is present-day Xi'an. Such a maritime route may well have been the transmission route of the Cinderella story.

The question is why then, if the transmission was from Thailand to China, the Yexian story tells it the other way round – a Chinese girl goes abroad to live on a distant foreign island after her shoe is transported there. Do not forget that this is a story told by the Zhuang people. The Zhuang narrator's integrity and cultural pride naturally made Zhuang culture the origin of the touching story. To the Zhuang narrator's mind, the girl's delicately hand-sewn shoe would be cherished as treasure by foreigners living as far as islands in the sea. The story that arrived in Guangxi from the seas was thus claimed to be a local story. Claude Levi-Strauss (1973: 7–23) insightfully noted that the principle of a tribe's myth was essentially based upon a psychological mechanism, that is, a desire to elevate the self-integrity of the tribal community. But the truth of the Yexian story is that it came from outside China, after hundreds of years of sojourning on the seas and along the coasts.

Yexian, the Festival, and the Blue Garment: A Zhuang Adaptation

Sailing from the island of Tuohan, the early Cinderella story once again accompanied its storytellers in navigating the oceanic waves to reach a seaport in northern Vietnam and then traveled northward to Nanning in

Guangxi where the Zhuang people lived. At that crossroads between Vietnam and China, the story once again adapted itself to local customs and cultures. In this region the so-called One Hundred Yue ethnic peoples (*baiyue* 百越) or Luoyue (Lạc Việt) people lived. They shared the common regional culture of Yue, but each ethnic community had its own distinctive lifestyle. Given the diverse but similar cultures in this region, it is impossible to identify the chronological order of the transmission of the Cinderella story here. Based on the materials collected, we will first discuss the Zhuang elements in the Yexian story, before we explore one of the five northern Vietnamese stories. (According to Ding [1994: 115–149], the Yexian story and the five northern Vietnamese stories share the same narrative ancestry.)

In the Yexian story, three quintessential Zhuang elements, and to some extent, characteristics of the shared cultures of the various ethnic groups in the Lingnan region, deserve mentioning: (1) the girl's name is Yexian; (2) the girl visits the local festival where her exquisitely made shoe leads to a blissful marriage; (3) the girl wears blue clothing with brilliant woven patterns.

First, the girl's name, Yexian, is spelled in pinyin which is the phonetic spelling of modern Mandarin. If pronounced in a reconstructed ancient Yue dialect spoken in the Guangxi region where the story circulated, her name would have been Yi Han. Ancient Zhuang people, and to some extent, the other ethnic peoples living in the region, used "yi" as a prefix to a girl's name. For example, the name "Yi Jia" in the Zhuang language and the name "Yi Dalao" in the language of the Dai people might have used different Han Chinese scripts to designate the sound of "yi." But the syllable "yi" in both the ethnic languages has the same meaning – "girl." Further, the first ruler of the ancient country of Funan 扶南 (located in mainland Southeast Asia, covering parts of present-day Cambodia, Thailand, and Vietnam) was a woman named "Yi Liu." Just from the prefix "yi" in her name, her gender is obvious (Nong, 1998: 42).

Second, the story was told by a person living in a "cave." The local festival the girl attends is called the "cave festival" (dongjie 洞節). The people from the place are called "cave people" (dongren 洞人). At the festival, the girl loses her shoe which leads to a blissful marriage. The word for "cave" does not indicate that these Indigenous people lived in actual caves; rather it was a word adopted by medieval Han imperial officials to designate the mountainous regions where ethnic peoples lived (Nong, 1998: 42). The Zhuang people have been known for their singing festival celebrated on the third day of the third month of the lunar calendar every year. At this festival, young women and men dress in their best clothes to participate in a contest in which they sing spontaneously to express their affection and feelings for their intended mates. Marriages are arranged after this festival. Thus, this is the festival where young people in the Zhuang community find love and lifelong companions. The girls wear their prettiest embroidered shoes that they make themselves to demonstrate their sewing and embroidery skills. If a girl likes a boy, she may throw him an "embroidered ball" – a traditional Zhuang-ethnic love token. A pair of shoes are also often given as a romantic gift. The Yexian story definitely affirms the general cultural pattern of the singing festival celebrated by the Zhuang community in Guangxi.

Third, the girl wears an indigo garment with brilliant, embroidered patterns. The Zhuang people have been known for centuries for making high-quality indigo cloth through their unique dying techniques. As depicted in Figure 26 in the "tributary painting" from the Qing dynasty, a Zhuang woman from the He 賀 county "wears a short shirt with brocaded borders and a delicately embroidered skirt made completely of brocade. She is accepting a scarf and a kerchief both of which are made of Zhuang brocade" (Tan, 2023: 14) (Figures 25–26).

To summarize, the Zhuang people in Guangxi instilled Zhuang culture into the story that came from outside. Out of integrity and cultural pride, the Zhuang people made their home the origin of the Yexian story.

Figure 25 Patterns in a Zhuang brocade (upper register); patterns in a Yao brocade (lower register). Guangxi Zhuangzu Zizhiqu gongyi meishu yanjiu suo, 1976: 2.

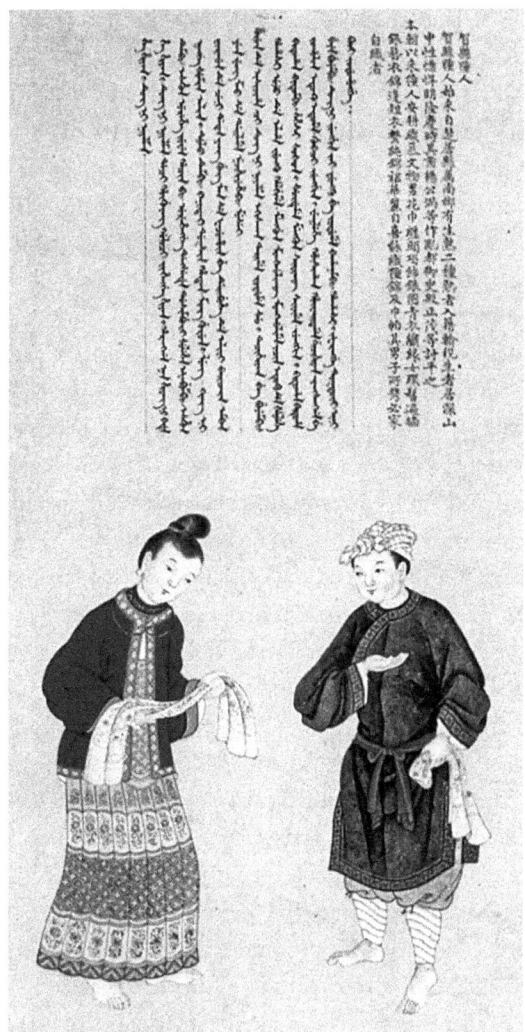

Figure 26 Images of Zhuang people in He county, Guangxi, from Xie Sui's *Tributary Painting of the Qing Empire*. The Zhuang woman portrayed in the painting is receiving a scarf as a romantic gift from the Zhuang man. The woman is wearing an indigo garment trimmed with brocades of brilliant colors and patterns. Her skirt is also made of intricate brocades in vivid hues. Wikipedia Commons.

The Deity and the Fish: A Vietnamese Adaptation

The story that circulated in northern Vietnam is very similar to the Yexian story in Guangxi, except that the king is a local sovereign, demonstrating again how the Cinderella tale always adapted itself to the local soil. The story dates back to the fourth century BCE and specifies that it took place in a village in Bac Ninh province of Vietnam that is only thirty kilometers from Hanoi. The girl's name is Cai-Tam. She has a stepmother and a stepsister, and she feeds a small fish which later grows into a splendid golden fish living in her backyard pond. After the fish dies, a deity appears to tell her to bury the fish bones under her bed. (In some versions, the deity is the Buddha or the Goddess of Compassion; Ding, 1994: 134). One day, the stepmother and her daughter happily go to a festival, leaving Cai-Tam behind, ordering her to stay home and sort beans. The deity helps Cai-Tam by telling some birds to do the tedious work for her. He also tells her to look under her bed, where Cai-Tam finds beautiful clothes, jewels, and gold shoes. In a blue and silver dress and golden shoes, Cai-Tam hurries to the festival. On her way, she drops one of her shoes. A courtier finds it and presents it to the prince. (In one version, when she hangs her shoe to dry, a crow flies down and carries it away to present to the sovereign.) Amazed at its exquisite craftsmanship and small size, the prince begins to search for its owner and decides to marry her. But as soon as Cai-Tam is successfully found, on the wedding day, the stepmother makes an excuse to ask Cai-Tam to go out to work and then dresses her own daughter as the bride to marry the prince. When Cai-Tam finds out, she commits suicide. Her soul is reincarnated into a bird that soars into the palace to sing in front of the prince to tell him of her misery. At the prince's request, the bird hides in his sleeve to demonstrate that it is the reincarnated Cai-Tam. When they hear of this, the stepmother and the stepsister both drown themselves. Just as in the Yexian story, both the stepmother and the stepsister turn into mournful spirits, and by their tomb a pagoda is erected in their memory (Ding, 1974: 25–27; 1994: 133).

Located in a coastal region, Bac Ninh province was the first Vietnamese area to come into contact with Buddhism from India. When Indian merchants traded cinnamon, pepper, and incense in central Vietnam, they also brought Buddhist and Hindu deities like Bodhisattva Avalokitesvara and Vishnu and Siva. When the Cinderella story arrived in the village in Bac Ninh, it flourished together with the Buddhist and Hindu stories. The well-known thousand-armed, thousand-eyed Bodhisattva Avalokitesvara statue in crimson and gilt wood, sculpted in 1656 and housed at the But Thap Temple in Bac Ninh, and the famous One Pillar Temple built in 1049 that enshrined Bodhisattva Avalokitesvara both attest to the popularity of the deity in northern Vietnam (Figure 27).

One element in this Vietnamese version stands out to prove the story's Buddhist influence: The deity that appears in front of Cai-Tam is a bodhisattva. The core concept of Mahayana Buddhism is to rescue people from wretched conditions. The earliest Chinese account on Bodhisattva Avalokitesvara or Guanyin, *A Record of the Proven Response of Bodhisattva*

Early Globalism and Chinese Literature 63

Figure 27 The thousand-armed, thousand-eyed Guanyin built in 1656, housed at But Thap Temple in Bac Ninh, Vietnam. Wikipedia Commons.

Avalokitesvara 光世音應驗記 by Fu Liang 傅亮 (374–426), reiterates, "Bodhisattva Avalokitesvara can grant wishes to people in this life. We should pray wholehcartedly" (Dong, 2002: 7). The story of Yexian, the little girl who found herself in a tragic situation and who prayed over the fish bones to make her wish come true, fits the gist of Mahayana Buddhism.

Further, Beauchamp has insightfully interpreted the golden fish in the Yexian story as a symbol of the Goddess of Compassion (also known as the Bodhisattva Avalokitesvara or Guanyin) – the deity that appears in front of Yexian. In her form as the Fish-Basket Avalokitesvara, she usually carries a basket of fish (Figures 28–29). This important detail is much clearer in the Vietnamese versions in which the deity is directly called the Buddha or the God of Compassion (Beauchamp, 2010: 476–480). In particular, it is true that the deity is described as having unkempt hair. In *Journey to the West*, the fish-basket

Figure 28 Zhao Mengfu's (1254–1322) painting of *The Fish-Basket Guanyin*. Dressed in plain garments, the bodhisattva holds prayer beads in one hand and a bamboo basket with two live carps in the other, exuding a calm, graceful composure. Courtesy of the National Palace Museum.

Guanyin indeed appears disheveled as she hurries to the human world to save Tripitaka.

After Guangxi and northern Vietnam, the story reached southern Vietnam, other mountainous borderlands of China, and central China where the tale was Sinicized. The story shows again its malleability. Modern Chinese versions are not quite as dramatic or raw as the original Zhuang version (Ding, 1974: 32–33). From China, it has been well documented that the story's variants gradually moved overland to Europe from 850 CE through the "Silk Road" trade routes (Dundes, 1982), but the *significant* way that this Yexian/Cinderella story traveled to Europe was by a relatively quick (two to three years-long) maritime route landing in the port of Venice of Italy in the sixteenth century. A radical version of the story about a girl named Doralice appears in the fairy-tale collection *The Pleasant Nights* by the Italian writer Giovanni Francesco Straparola (c. 1485–1558). Later, a major version of the Cinderella story,

Figure 29 In the Tran Quoc Pagoda (built in the sixth century) in Hanoi, Vietnam, goldfish were swimming in the man-made pond where the Guanyin figurine is placed atop of rocky mountains. The scene symbolizes Guanyin's compassion and the significance of releasing captive animals. Photograph by Yuanfei Wang.

"The Cinderella Cat," with the missing shoe motif, by Giambattista Basile (1575–1632) spread across Europe. Likely, both Straparola and Basile learned the story from various "Oriental" sources floating around the seaports of Venice and Naples (Zipes, 2000). From Italy, the story flourished and continued into Germany, France, and England.[22]

Of course, we all know about the glass shoe in the English version. But the received opinion is that the slipper was originally made of fur, called *vair* in French, as the French versions show. But in the process of translation and transmission across Europe, the word *vair* was mistaken as the French word *verre*, or glass (Ralston, 1982: 37–38). This beautiful mistake became the staple of the Cinderella story that has lasted up to the present. Since the story of the glass slipper has been repeated endlessly, we will end this account here.

---

[22] We thank Fay Beauchamp for sending her insightful note on the spread of the story from China to Europe via maritime routes.

Concluding Remarks

The global dissemination of the Cinderella story during the Middle Ages represents a significant, widespread, cross-cultural literary diffusion. It is a fascinating example of medieval world literature. While we started the voyage of the Cinderella story at Greece, the story made a major transformation in India and continued to evolve in Southeast Asia, China, and Europe. This illustrates that the Cinderella story does not have a single point of origin but has multiple points of origin.

The simple story about a girl's lost shoe that is intricately small and beautiful, her rivalry with her siblings, and her miraculous social ascendance has captivated audiences worldwide. The story's global popularity can be attributed to its ability to tap into the universal human condition that is concerned with the girl's anxieties in her adolescent years and how she handles malice and ill will in difficult situations. The story promises the girl ultimate gratification and unique personal achievement once she endures hardships and undertakes difficult tasks (Bettelheim, 2010: 276). But what adds to the story's allure is its remarkable chameleon-like ability to adapt to its environment and move across boundaries, in myriad ways.

5 Voyages of Zheng He: The World in Ming Literature

In the preceding section, the literary diffusion of the early renditions of the Cinderella story unfolded in a direct and expansive manner – the story traveled from one port to another worldwide and settled into local soil through adaptation. Those who embraced and modified the story did not have to venture overseas for source materials. Rather, the story reached them through diverse channels. Akin to the case of the Cinderella story, another form of literary diffusion in premodern China also verges upon large-scale literary representation and imaginative depictions of the external world at the local level. But in this type of literary diffusion, the new knowledge is not limited to a singular tale but encompasses a wealth of information that represents the globalized world in its entirety.

The example in question pertains to the Ming literature depicting Admiral Zheng He's seven voyages on the Indian Ocean between 1405 and 1433. The voyages reached as far as the east African coast. The three translators who accompanied Zheng He to travel overseas composed three travelogues to record the information of the countries visited, namely *Records of the Western Oceanic Countries* 西洋番國志 (1434), *The Overall Survey of the Star Raft* 星槎勝覽 (1436), and *The Overall Survey of the Ocean's Shores* 瀛涯勝覽 (1451). Through wood-block commercial printing at such cosmopolitan cities as Nanjing and Hangzhou, these three travelogues were widely circulating in the late Ming society, projecting the Ming people's curiosity toward Southeast Asia, South Asia, the Middle East, and Africa. Further, the variety drama *Sanbao's Heaven-Ordained Voyages on the Western Ocean* 奉天命三寶下西洋 (hereafter, *Heaven-Ordained Voyages*, c. sixteenth century) by a court dramatist and Luo Maodeng's vernacular fiction *Eunuch Sanbao's Voyages on the Indian Ocean* 三寶太監西洋記通俗演義 (hereafter *Eunuch Sanbao*, 1592) represent the two major extant literary depictions of Admiral Zheng He's voyages across the Indian Ocean. Whereas the drama was aimed at a royal audience at court, the vernacular fiction was published through a commercial press in Nanjing for a wider audience in the cosmopolitan city. The authors of the Ming literature on Zheng He never traveled overseas. They obtained all their knowledge of the world indirectly by reading the world travelogues and histories that were readily available to them through the commercial book market or through secondhand information that circulated in the imperial palace and Ming society. To this end, we will term such literary diffusion and representation of large-scale world knowledge as "indirect literary diffusion." This section will hence identify several important techniques of indirect literary diffusion employed in the two works through which the narrators delineate the world and the readers imagine the globe.

Geraldine Heng has observed that medieval "travel romance" writings, like *Mandeville's Travels* (1357–1371), specialize in bringing those "far-flung objects, places, peoples, and events" home (Heng 2003: 250).[23] The works *Heaven-Ordained Voyages* and *Eunuch Sanbao* are the Chinese *Mandeville's Travels*. In their storytelling, the world in the distance – generally termed as the Western Ocean – is projected back at home as if it were a "mirror of the Western Ocean" (*Xiyang jing* 西洋鏡, the Chinese translation of the "peep show" – an early form of cinema that became popular in China at the end of the eighteenth century and showed vignettes and anecdotes of the world's far-flung ports). The prototype of this world panorama can be traced, at least in part, to the three world travelogues that systematically list the visited "western oceanic countries" and to the subgenre of Chinese paintings known as *Portraits of Periodic Offering* 職貢圖 (Figure 30).

Much like the "mirror of the Western Ocean" or the *Portraits of Periodic Offering*, *Heaven-Ordained Voyages* and *Sanbao Eunuch* offered vignettes, glimpses, and anecdotes of the exotic world to their Chinese audience. This textual heterotopia conferred pleasure and power, as well as criticism of the Chinese "I," a collective, abstract "I" that was shared between the Chinese novel

---

[23] The book chapter "Eye on the World: Mandeville's Pleasure Zones; or, Cartography, Anthropology, and Medieval Travel Romance" in *Empire of Magic: Medieval Romance and the Politics of Cultural Fantasy* by Geraldine Heng has inspired this section's overall understanding of the world in the Ming literature on Zheng He.

Figure 30 A Song dynasty duplicate of the Yuan emperor of Liang Dynasty (502–557) Xiao Yi's 蕭繹 (508–555) *Portraits of Periodic Offering*. In the painting, each ambassador represents one foreign country. From right to left, the envoys in the first segment were the Hephthalites, Persia, Korea, Kucha, Japan, and in the second segment were Malaysia, Qiang, Yarkand, Kabadiyan, Kumedh, Balkh, and Merv. Wikipedia Commons.

readers or theater viewers and the literary narrator. On their virtual tour with Zheng He's armada, the audience was expected to identify with Zheng He's fleets as they followed him to venture into the exotic world.

An Ocean of Exotica at the Court

Heaven-Ordained Voyages was originally a *zaju* ("variety drama") in the form of a handwritten manuscript that circulated within the imperial palace of the Ming. Later it was collected by Ming literatus Zhao Qimei (1563–1624) and included in the *Maiwang Library's Edition of Zaju Old and New*. The anonymous author was likely a musician in the Bureau of Drums and Bells or the Bureau of Music in the imperial palace.

A court play such as this that was performed inside the imperial palace naturally catered to the emperor and royalty. As would be expected, it exhibits a Sinocentric tributary worldview. It begins with a palace command introducing the Western Ocean as a treasure trove and describing how all the maritime countries admired the virtues of the Ming emperor. It goes on to say that they were all striving to present their most valuable indigenous products as tribute to China to express their admiration of Chinese civilization, to form a diplomatic and trade relationship with China, and to show their desire to be Sinicized. But the vast ocean obstructed communications.

The first technique of portraying the world, as manifested in the *Heaven-Ordained Voyages*, is delineating a visionary landscape of the world. The Ming court dramatist imagined a visionary cartography of the littoral countries that he intended to share with his royal audience. Such a narrative cartography blended individual visions with the contemporary cultural discourses of Southeast Asia, South Asia, the Middle East, and Africa.

The drama evinces the author-narrator's perspective of the Ming empire's positioning in the globalized world. Mixing fantasy and history, *Heaven-Ordained Voyages* portrays a few major ports that Zheng He's armada frequented during the seven voyages. In their narrative order, they are Guli 古里,[24] Java, Banda, Champa, Mecca, Sulu, Pahang, and a fantastic kingdom named the "Country of Penetrated Hearts," a variation on the "Country of Penetrated Chests" recorded in the Chinese mythological account *The Classic of Mountains and Seas* (Shanhai jing 山海經).[25]

Why these places? Guli, Champa, Java, and Mecca are significant and memorable sites in the history of Zheng He's voyages. In history, Guli and Champa were among the first stops of the voyages and Java and Mecca were major destinations. Zheng He visited Guli on every voyage, and he passed away there in 1433 on his way back to China. As for Champa, on the first visit, the Yongle emperor (1360–1424) gave the king of Champa the Great Ming calendar as a gift to make an alliance with Champa. In Java, the major island of the powerful Majapahit empire in the history of Indonesia and Southeast Asia, Zheng He and his followers visited the seaports of Durban in central Java (present-day Semarang), Gresik, Surabaya, Majapahit, and Canggu. During his visits, Zheng He also captured the Chinese pirate Chen Zuyi and pacified the "rebellion" of Chinese emigrants and merchants in the Old Port (present-day Palembang) (Figure 31). Mecca was among the furthest stops on Zheng He's voyages, together with Mogadishu/Xamar, Juba, and Brava along the coast of east Africa and Hormuz in the Persian Gulf. In Mecca, Zheng He and his crew drew an architectural painting of the Muslim holy site the Kaaba and visited the sultan of Mecca who dispatched diplomats to follow Zheng He's fleets back to the Ming court to visit the Ming emperor (Ma, 1970: 177–178).

But surprisingly, *Heaven-Ordained Voyages* features a small country named Sulu. Sulu is not as significant as Guli, Champa, Java, and Mecca, but the Ming playwright must have been quite familiar with Sulu's geographical importance and its diplomatic history with China, its produce, and its piratical activities when

---

[24] In history, Guli was located on the southwestern coast of India, in the Kerala region, and also known historically as Zamorin.
[25] Pahang is in the eastern sea coast of the Malaysia Peninsula. It was a vassal state of the country of Guli on the west coast of India.

Figure 31 A statue of Zheng He and a temple dedicated to him at Sam Po Kong, Semarang, Indonesia. Photograph by Yuanfei Wang.

he composed the play. Likely, the touching diplomatic story about the Sulu king's loyalty to China and the Yongle emperor's benevolence to his distant oceanic neighbor marked Sulu's distinctiveness in the play's visionary landscape of the Indian Ocean. In history, the three kings of Sulu, accompanied by their wives, children, and subordinates (altogether 340 people), undertook a maritime voyage to arrive in China to receive the sanction of the Yongle emperor who conferred upon them a seal, an edict, a crown, a belt, a horse with a saddle, and a scepter. But the Eastern Sulu king, Badugebahala (Chinese transliteration of the Sulu name), died at Dezhou in Shandong on his way back to his home country. To show his benevolence toward this foreign king who demonstrated his great loyalty to China, Yongle permitted him be buried at Dezhou and allowed his family to stay in China to observe three years of mourning before returning home. The Yongle emperor also appointed the Eastern Sulu king's son Dumahan as the new king of Eastern Sulu (Yan, 1993: 314–316).

In the play, the king of Sulu – played by a male supporting actor – accompanied by two Sulu officials, ascends the stage and delivers the following lines to the audience:

> The oceanic mist just dispersed, the morning sun is shining. Giant waves and high tides rest at the beaches. Having been living on the ocean for long,

Early Globalism and Chinese Literature 71

barbarians and mountain chieftains enjoy peace. I am the king of Sulu. My name is Badugebasuli (Chinese transliteration of his Sulu name). My father is the eastern king of Sulu, Badugebadala. These two, Jilabu and Jiladu, are the heads of my subordinates. In my country, everyone is brave and strong. Adjacent to the ocean, our islands are surrounded with dangerous cliffs. Although our fields are barren, we grow corn and wheat which could fill our belly. Sand whiting can also satiate us. We boil the sea to make salts, brew sugarcane juice into alcohol. We cook snails and clams as food and weave bamboo fibers into cloth. We also have spotted hawksbills and giant pearls. We have everything except two: colorful silk and porcelain bowls. (Xu, 1962: 33)

This way, the role introduces to the audience the Sulu king's name, his lineage, his officials, his people, Sulu's geography, food, and produce. These lines are adapted from a section on Sulu in Fei Xin's *Overall Survey of the Starry Raft* (Figure 32).

Sulu formed an important economic nexus in the main sea lanes linking China to Melaka, Java, and Maluku (Ptak, 1992: 28; Sutherland, 2011, 174). Because of its strategic position on the sea, the region near Sulu had always been known for its rampant piratical activities for centuries. Based upon this history of Sulu, the playwright humorously portrays the king of Sulu, the king of Pahang, and the king of the Country of Penetrated Hearts as pirates conspiring to hijack Zheng He's fleets to plunder the silk and porcelain from China. When they confront Zheng He and demand that he give them porcelain pieces as "fees for passage," a type of extortion, Zheng He generously presents each of them a "little porcelain tree" 小磁器的樹兒, telling them that Chinaware, like fruits, flowers, and leaves, grows on a "porcelain tree." He invites them to board his ships to appreciate more "porcelain trees." The men, depicted as naïve and ignorant "barbarians," believe Zheng He's story and get on the ships. Zheng He

Figure 32 Images of Sulu people from the *Portraits of the Periodic Offering of the Qing Empire*. Courtesy of Bibliothèque nationale de France.

then captures them and interrogates them for hijacking the fleets. The three kings all make excuses for themselves – the king of the Country of Penetrated Hearts justifies his actions because he "has no heart"; the king of Pahang promises to give Zheng He a load of crabs as compensation; and the king of Sulu explains that as a "barbarian," naturally, he engages in plundering. Eventually, all three kings promise to subordinate their kingdoms to China as vassal states. The play's depiction of these kings as pirates is thus superimposed upon the historical reality of Sulu's rampant piratical activities and its diplomatic history with China.

A second technique in portraying the world is to focus on depicting exotica which then becomes a synecdoche for the world. The structure of desire in *Heaven-Ordained Voyages* pivots on gathering exotic treasures and, specifically, luxury goods frequently traded on the seas. Obtaining precious goods epitomizes the exercise of power over the countries where the valuables originate. Treasures embody both the official and private maritime trade between China and Southeast Asia (Wan, 2005, 34). They are emblematic of the Western Ocean for the Ming playwright, his court audience, and to some extent, Ming society.

The exotica featured in the play are not randomly chosen. They all have historical and cultural references. Frequently traded economic goods such as coral trees, glass vases, agarwood, and Western Ocean (Southeast Asia) cloth mingle with precious gems such as sapphires, rubies, opals, night-illuminating pearls, and even a legendary and imaginary object – a "glow-in-the-dark" curtain. The night-illuminating pearls, for instance, may refer to the famous saltwater pearls near Sulu. "There is a pool filled with pearls. In the evening, light glows on the water surface. Native people trade pearls with the Chinese and gain profits of twenty- or thirtyfold on the biggest pearls" (Zhang, 1974: vol. 200, 11). The largest pearls on record measured up to one inch in diameter. One such pearl could sell for 700–800 taels of silver, as recorded in the *Overall Survey of the Starry Raft*. During their visit to China, the Sulu kings presented a giant pearl that weighed seven ounces and five *qian* – it greatly pleased the Yongle emperor. As for the precious gems, they frequently appear in the three travelogues: Gresik in Java and Ceylon (Sri Lanka) produced *yagu* and opals (Fei, 1954: 14); opals, sapphires, and rubies could be found in Hormuz; and in Aden, Zheng He bought a large opal, giant pearls, *yagu*, and coral trees (Gong, 2000: 35). By contrast, the luminous curtain – probably a curtain made of stringed pearls – was a more poetically fantastical object. It is not related to the history of Zheng He but can easily stir readers' imagination. An anecdote in the *Miscellaneous Records from the Pine Window* (*Songchuang zalu* 松窗雜錄) has it that a student used a luminous curtain from Jilin prefecture (a vassal state of the Tang dynasty in the south central part of the Korean peninsula) as a bribe for the ninth daughter of a local king to get her to plead with her father to release Prime Minister Yao. Another fantastical object staged in the drama is a mermaid's scarf wrapped around the neck of a foreign king who is dressed in a Mongolian *yesa* robe on which a dragon is embroidered. The "mermaid's scarf" was made of silk woven by mermaids in the legend.

Notably, this visionary world is centered around China. Their cultural confidence allowed the Chinese to take great pleasure in their appreciation of all sorts of exotica. The home and center of the world was always the imperial palace of the Ming. The exotic objects represented alterity and otherness. The subject – the Chinese "I" – however, never actually "needed" any exotica, except to observe it from a distance with pleasure, because "I" was awesomely independent and ordained by Heaven.

Mapping the World on the Printed Book

In 1592, Luo Maodeng published the vernacular novel *Eunuch Sanbao* through the *Shide Tang* publishing house in Nanjing. The author explains in the preface that Hideyoshi's invasion of Korea caused him to turn his eyes to the ocean and rethink Ming China's recent maritime history – Zheng He's seven voyages.

Eunuch Sanbao fantasizes a globalized world that the Chinese Muslim Admiral Zheng He and his armada conquer and dominate. The novel begins with the Yongle emperor's command to search for the missing imperial jade seal which the last Yuan (Mongol) emperor took with him as he fled to the Indian Ocean. Yet this search for the jade seal always leads to Zheng He's armada waging wars with foreign countries. China always wins these battles waged by the armada, and the "barbarian kingdoms" are obliged to acknowledge China's supreme position in the world and submit as vassal states. Paradoxically, this triumphant vision of China is rooted in late Ming literati's anxieties over Ming China's weakened imperial identity. Threats from the sea – Hideyoshi's invasion of Korea and the powerful Chinese maritime merchant-pirates, represented by Lin Daoqian (died in 1580) and Wang Zhi (1501–1560), contesting with the land-based Ming state – generated vigorous discussions on pirates and the seas in the late Ming (Wang, 2021).

Anxiety, uncertainty, curiosity about the outside world, and pleasure in writing and reading helped channel knowledge of the world through the publication of *Eunuch Sanbao*. Geographical, cultural, religious, and scientific information about the world, blended with imagination and moral inculcation, can all be found in the novel. The Chinese "I" in the novel – from the perspective of the author-narrator and his Chinese characters – finds itself having to face and delineate the world in its broadest sense.

The world envisioned in *Eunuch Sanbao* is much larger than that in *Heaven-Ordained Voyages*. *Eunuch Sanbao* maps out its vision of the globe. Zheng He's armada reached dozens of countries and islands in the Indian Ocean, including Champa, Panduranga, Siam, Java, the Country of Women, Sumatra, Malacca, Safa (possibly Sohar), the Maldives, Kollam, Cochin, Calicut, Golden Eye, Xigela,[26] Mogadishu, Juba, Brava, Hormuz, Silver Eye, Aden, Mecca, and the netherworld. Among them, the Country of Women, Golden Eye, Silver Eye, and the netherworld are, of course, spaces of imagination or religious belief.

Despite the fictional elements, *Eunuch Sanbao* is intimately connected to geographical and historical writing. The major difference between *Eunuch Sanbao* and other similar full-length vernacular novels on world travel such as *Journey to the West* and *Flowers in the Mirror* 鏡花緣 (1828) is that *Eunuch Sanbao* deliberately represents the secular world in its entirety in a realistic way as it purposefully amasses and compiles diverse phenomena and information. The novel intentionally catalogues foreign cultures and countries through enumerating their differences in weather, geography, economy, agriculture, language, culture, customs, clothing, hairstyle, law, produce, and funeral and marriage rituals, among many other subjects. This is the third technique of portraying the world.

The fourth technique of portraying the world involves vernacular paraphrases of existing travelogues. For example, before his fleets reached Mecca, Zheng He arrived on the east coast of Africa. In Mogadishu, Juba, and Brava, *Eunuch Sanbao* once again paints an imaginary vignette of the Chinese–African encounter: The houses in the African cities are built with stones. The earth is barren without grass or trees. Because it may not rain for several years, the wells have to be extremely deep in order to reach underground water. The people make sheepskins into portable water bags. In Brava, people make a living by producing sea salt. Through a sentinel, Zheng He also learns that all the men in Mogadishu, Juba, and Brava have curly long hair and they wear a piece of cloth wrapped around their waist. The women tie their hair on top of their head and wear stringed earrings and a long silver necklace with tassels that reach the chest. Outdoors, they wrap a cloth around their body and cover their face with a blue gauze fabric. They also wear leather shoes. This vernacular description of Eastern African culture and customs paraphrases a classical-language passage from *The Overall Survey of the Star Raft*. The vernacular paraphrasing includes usage of vernacular grammar (such as some adverbs and prepositions) and a question-and-answer conversation between the inquisitive Zheng He and the sentinel.

Similarly, when Zheng He's armada reaches Mecca, the narrator describes the landmark Kaaba:

---

[26] Tansen Sen believes that this geographical name may be an error in historical accounts.

When they reached the Paradise Temple, they saw that it was divided into four wings, each of which had ninety rooms. White-jade pillars supported each room and yellow jade was used to pave the ground. The main hall was built with five-colored marble stones. The temple looked like a cube. On top of its flat roof was another roof. Like a pagoda, it had nine layers in total. A stone tablet was erected in front of the hall that was one *zhang* high and one *chi* wide. (Luo, 1984: 2342)

Several preexisting travelogues could be the textual references for this paragraph including *The Overall Survey of the Star Raft* and Luo Yuejiong's *Records of All Guests* (1592).

Eunuch Sanbao's vernacular element indicates that the novel was intended for readers who did not look down on the use of vernacular language or non-Chinese knowledge. Its readership was wide, ranging from higher elites to lesser elites, merchants, and women, reaching the wider segments of late Ming society. These readers had a strong appetite for new and exotic information rather than just orthodox knowledge and moral principles such as that found in the Confucian canon. The novel was a product of the thriving commercial publishing in the late Ming (Chow, 2004; Meyer-Fong, 2007: 787–817). The quickly expanding printing centers in Nanjing, Hangzhou, and Jianyang offered the large reading population opportunities to read about non-Chinese societies and cultures, even though, as would be expected, such knowledge was always a mixture of fact and fantasy.

In the novel, the Chinese "I" seems always to find itself challenged and rebutted by the "barbarian" Other, partly because the claim of searching for the lost jade seal cannot justify the repeated invasion of foreign territories and is met with resistance, and partly because the genre of the novel often projects conflicting and subversive voices from different social groups (Bakhtin, 1982: 273–331). Resistance and conflict also indicate the narrator's conflicted attitude toward invasion, perhaps demonstrating a latent respect for foreign cultures and states and a rooted belief in peace. For example, in Mogadishu, Zheng He's fleets again meet local resistance. The Honorable Tuoluo, abbot of the Flying Dragon Buddhist Temple in the African port city, convinces his fellow countrymen to fight back against Zheng He's invasion: "Our country is hundreds of thousands of *li* from China. Out of the blue, they come to conquer us. They may think we are a small country, but we have countless excellent archers." He sends the commander-in-chief, Yunmu Kouche, to Zheng He's camp to demonstrate his superior archery skills in order to convince the Chinese not to attempt to conquer Mogadishu.

However, the Chinese "I" recurrently employs Confucian ethnic values to counter the resistance of the so-called barbarians. Seeing that Yunmu Kouche can shoot the target perfectly, the Chinese martial champion Tang argues that simply shooting the target is not enough to win. It is "winning the opponent's heart" that matters. He proclaims, "We Chinese take trust and righteousness as our foundation." With this, he throws his spear and hits the African general, but the weapon does not hurt him. With this example, the narrator demonstrates that China wins its battles not by violence but by morality.

It seems axiomatic that the novel would envision a Sinocentric world where the Chinese self is moral, authentic, and civilized while the barbarian "other" is immoral and uncivilized. But even within this Sinocentric framework, the narrator offers positive and even idealistic views of non-Confucian religions and cultures. This represents the fifth technique for portraying the world. For instance, Zheng He's sentinel concludes that the cultural customs in the East African countries are "honest" and "genuine." Similar observations are made regarding Cochin (in India), Nagur in Sumatra, Mecca, Java, Minangkabau in West Sumatra, and "Xigela." "The further west, the richer the countries are, and the more civilized the people become" (Luo, 1984: 2701). Zheng He and his entourage also show immense respect to Islam and Buddhism. In Mecca, the Muslim admiral pays homage to the Kaaba. In Ceylon and elsewhere, sacred Buddhist sites and legends mesmerize these Chinese voyagers: Zheng He visits a monastery in Ceylon that enshrines the Buddha's tooth and relics.

Importantly, this indirect literary diffusion demonstrates a need to satisfy the Chinese self's curiosity for the strange, the weird, and the unusual. As a result, exotic customs are frequently described. The men from Nagur of Sumatra always tattoo their faces with patterns of fauna and flora. Artistes train tigers to perform in circuses in East Africa. In Surabaya (Indonesia), when a woman hopes to have children, she will bring liquor, fruits, meat, and pastry to visit an old male monkey living in the forest who leads tens of thousands of long-tail monkeys. In Pahang, local people observe a "bizarre" custom. They carve aromatic wood into puppets and use human blood as a sacrifice to the wooden dolls. These divine figurines will then grant them what they are praying for. In some other cultures, the people are far more pious and devout than the Chinese. The Minangkabau people in West Sumatra honor their relatives and the elderly on a daily basis. The younger members of the family bring wine and food to the home of the elderly if they have not seen them for a day. In Belitung, wives are extremely loyal to their husbands. After her husband passes away, a woman shaves her head, destroys her face with a knife, and fasts for seven days and seven nights. Then she commits suicide by walking into the fire in which her husband's corpse is being cremated.

Both the readers and the characters in *Eunuch Sanbao* find the countless types of exotica presented as tribute to Zheng He charming: The Chinese "I" is enraptured. The seemingly endless lists of tribute presented to China in

Eunuch Sanbao – recorded after numerous encounters with foreign countries – reveal a profound motivation to catalogue, even exhaustively enumerate, every conceivable type of world exotica, organizing them (or at least their names) as if the novel were an encyclopedia.

In the narrative's infatuated depictions and endless lists, the exotic items appear mythical and magical. The "Sea Mirror" is the name of a certain kind of scallop or oyster. When asked about this whimsical name, Zheng He explains that it is because the shells shine when they reflect sunlight. A kind of incense is called "White Crane Incense" because the incense smoke transforms into a pair of white cranes that soar into the sky. A kind of date-like fruit is called "how-so" because the berries can only be harvested once every 900 years. Since no human being can live long enough to witness the flower becoming fruit, people give the berries the curious name.

Eunuch Sanbao portrays many fearless foreign female warriors. Their stunning martial arts intimidate the Chinese men. Witch Wang from the kingdom of Bolin near Java can "thrust through the ocean to make a way." She fights staunchly to the death for her Javanese husband by the name of Gnaw Sea Dry. In contrast, Yellow Balsam from the Country of Women marries the Chinese martial champion Tang. This female warrior loyal to China helps the Chinese armada to fight against its foreign opponents, teaches the Chinese to perform magic, and in Aden, cleverly steals into the storehouse of the Aden king and procures mountains of silver and gold for the Chinese ship. She then returns to China with her husband where the emperor bestows upon her the title of Lady of the Second Rank. These brave women are also extremely outspoken: They not only criticize the Chinese armada for invading their homeland but also constantly berate the Chinese men for looking down upon women. "Slave! Your silence divulges your contempt for women! Do you not know that Nüwa who smelted the five-colored stones to patch the broken sky and Mulan who enlisted in the army on behalf of her father are both women!" These women are also imagined as sexually dangerous. The queen of the Country of Women, who admires Chinese civilization, wants to have intercourse with Zheng He, but there is a priceless moment when she finds out that he is a eunuch. The legendary fatal diseases – sores and infections – caused by intercourse between a woman from the Country of Women and a man from the Western Ocean indicate the danger and lure of the seas that beckon the tempted voyagers.

However, not all exotica, foreign religions and cultures, and foreign creatures are wholeheartedly appreciated and accepted by the Chinese emperor in the novel:

> The thirty-second country to present tribute is Baraawe (a port city in present-day Somalia). . . . The Eunuch of Attendants reads the list of tribute: "A jade

Buddha, a pair of jade tablets, a pair of jade pillows, two pairs of cat's eye stones, two pairs of emeralds, one pair of Arabian oryxes, one pair of zebras, two pairs of lions, one pair of leopards, ten rhino horns, fifty elephant tusks, ten boxes of ambergris, two thousand gold coins, five thousand silver coins, ten loads of aromatic rice, and ten bundles of fragrant vegetables." After taking a look, the emperor says, "We cannot disrespect the Buddha statue. Put it in the Waguan Temple and make offerings to it. As for the animals such as the Arabian oryxes, zebras, lions, and leopards, although we can easily obtain them, it is actually very hard to raise them and keep them alive. From now on, do not procure these kinds of animals. Give the fragrant rice and vegetables to farmers and gardeners to grow in the fields." All the civil and military ministers in the court believe that, "enshrining the jade Buddha statue is to revere ghosts and deities. Worrying about difficulties of rearing the oryxes, zebras, lions, and leopards is to prevent tyranny in rulership. Giving seeds to farmers and gardeners is to make agriculture and people the foundation of the society." (Luo, 1984: 2707)

What this paragraph shows is that the variety and complexity of the world can only be appreciated *selectively* and *metaphorically*. The Buddha statue and the exotic grains and plants can be kept and recognized in China, whereas the rare beasts have to be turned away. This is because the emperor considers his society fundamentally agricultural and one in which land is prioritized over the sea. On land, agriculture and religion are much more significant than rare animal species that not only do not provide for the people but could send a dangerous metaphorical message to the society and the emperor.

Concluding Remarks

Both the *Heaven-Ordained Voyages* and *Eunuch Sanbao* constructed a global world in its totality. The techniques employed in their portrayal of the world include (1) delineating a visionary landscape; (2) depicting exotica as a synecdoche for the world; (3) deliberately representing the secular world in its entirety in a realistic way as it purposefully amasses and compiles diverse phenomena and information; (4) paraphrasing in the vernacular the existing travelogues on the world; and (5) envisioning a Sinocentric world. This indirect literary diffusion is an act of appropriating existing information through reading, paraphrasing, and recreation. Essentially, indirect literary diffusion is an act of storytelling – telling stories about the world, at home – in the imperial palace or a cosmopolitan city.

Epilogue

The stories told in *Early Globalism and Chinese Literature* have been around us for hundreds and thousands of years. Likely, they will remain a part of our lives forever. What made these tales timeless and ubiquitous, as they migrated from one culture to another? We hope we have shown that religious beliefs, visions, the inclination for virtues, compassion, and salvation, pleasure in reading, writing, and storytelling, anxieties, curiosity, the will to persevere, simplicity, adaptability, and the agency of languages and images all fueled the endless global movements of these age-old stories.

This Element proposes to explore "early globalism and Chinese literature" through the lens of "literary diffusion." The first form of literary diffusion discussed is Buddhist literary diffusion. Chinese culture welcomed Buddhism from India and Central Asia, leading to a profound revolutionary influence on Chinese language and literature. The second form of literary diffusion, known as facilitated diffusion, engages Chinese literature with the world. Facilitated diffusion undergirds how oceans, Southeast Asia, and other traditionally overlooked regions and cultures have played a pivotal role in developing Chinese literature.

Globalism has a rich history predating modernity. China and Chinese literature have always been connected with the world at large, never existing in isolation. Medieval global literary diffusion has left a lasting imprint on Chinese language, literature, and culture. The timeless tales highlighted in this Element – the burning house parable, the tale of Mahamaudgalyayana's rescue of his mother from the underworld, the "journey to the West" stories, the Yexian/Cinderella narratives, and the literary accounts of Admiral Zheng He's maritime voyages – are just a handful of the numerous luminous seashells washed ashore by the tides of early global history. These tokens of time connect us with the past and the future.

Appendix

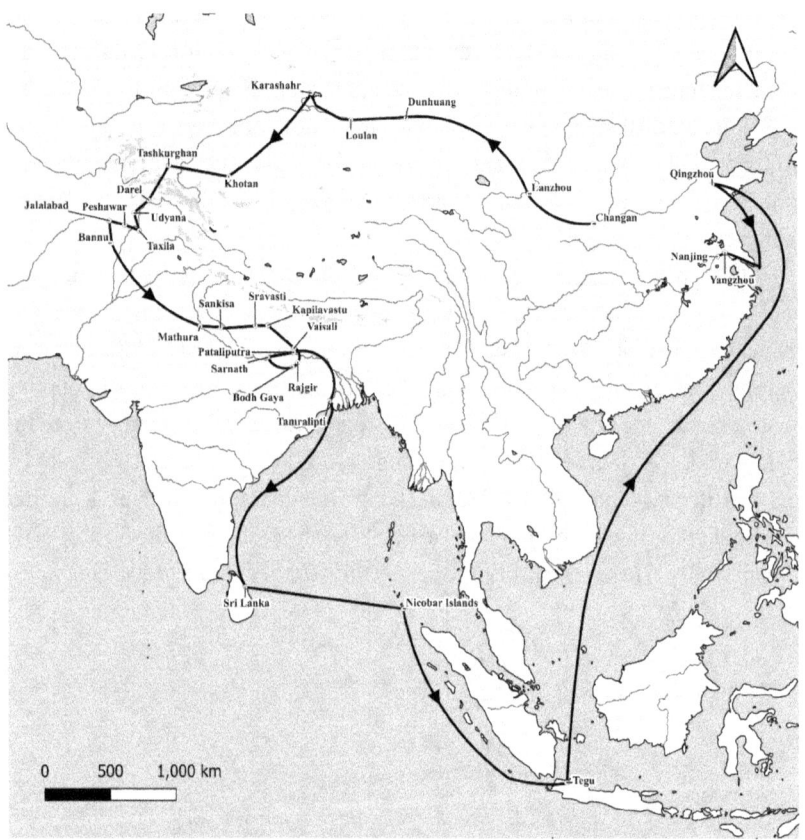

Figure A1 The desert–sea loop illustrates Faxian's routes from China to India overland and back to China by sea. Map drawn by Man Po Wong. This figure is also available in the online resources (www.cambridge.org/earlyglobalism).

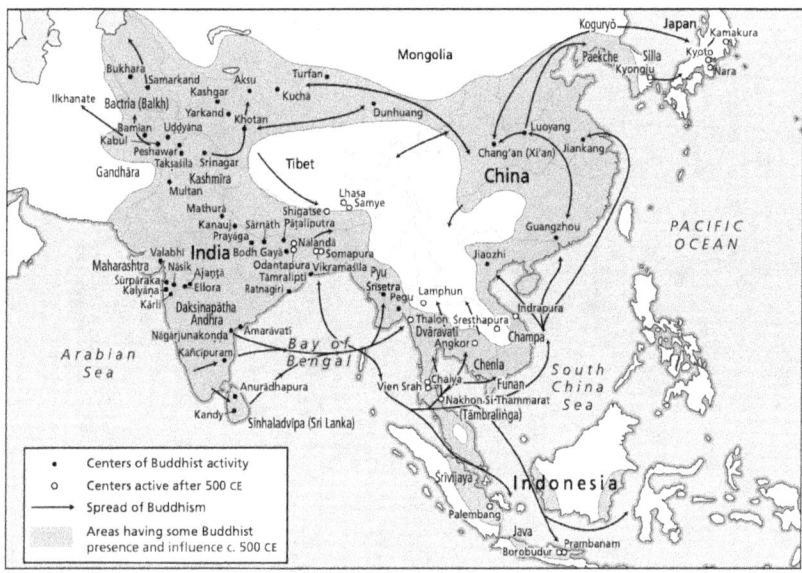

Figure A2 The spread of Buddhism in Asia. Source: Sen, 2015: 449. Courtesy of Cambridge University Press. This figure is also available in the online resources (www.cambridge.org/earlyglobalism).

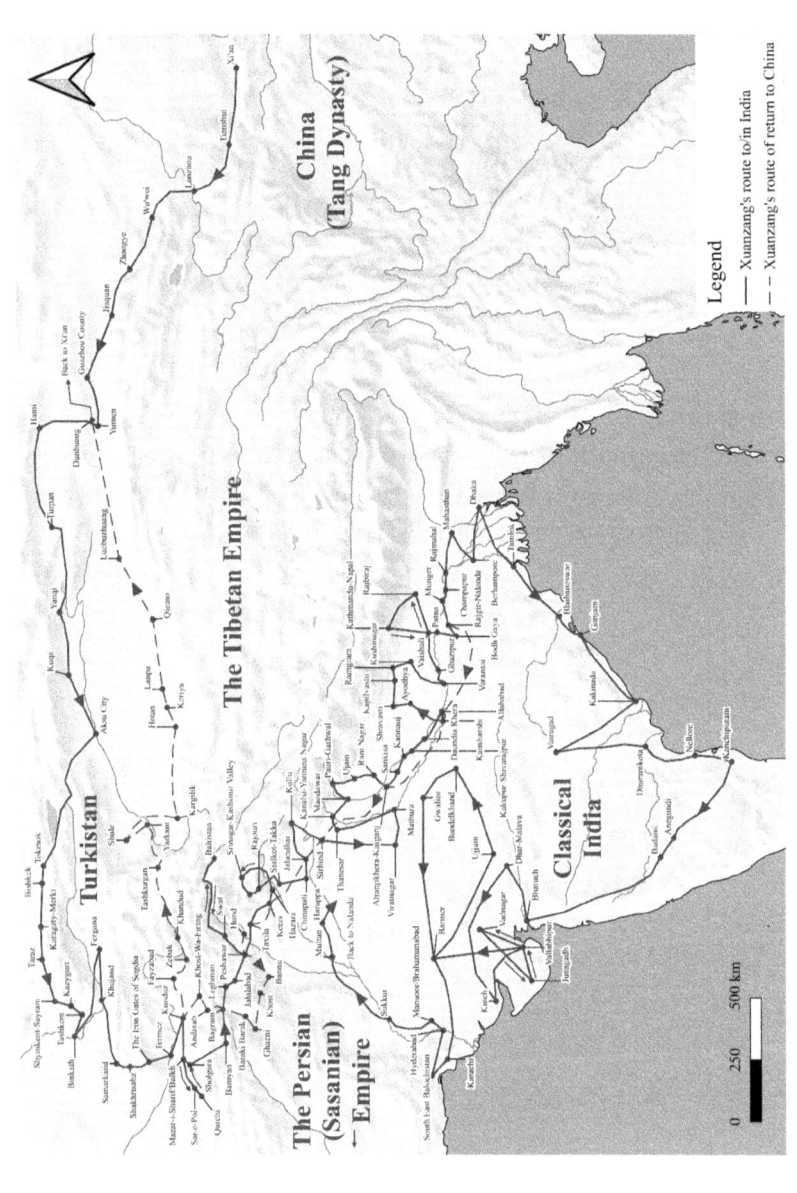

Figure A3 The itinerary of Xuanzang. Map drawn by Man Po Wong. This figure is also available in the online resources (www.cambridge.org/earlyglobalism).

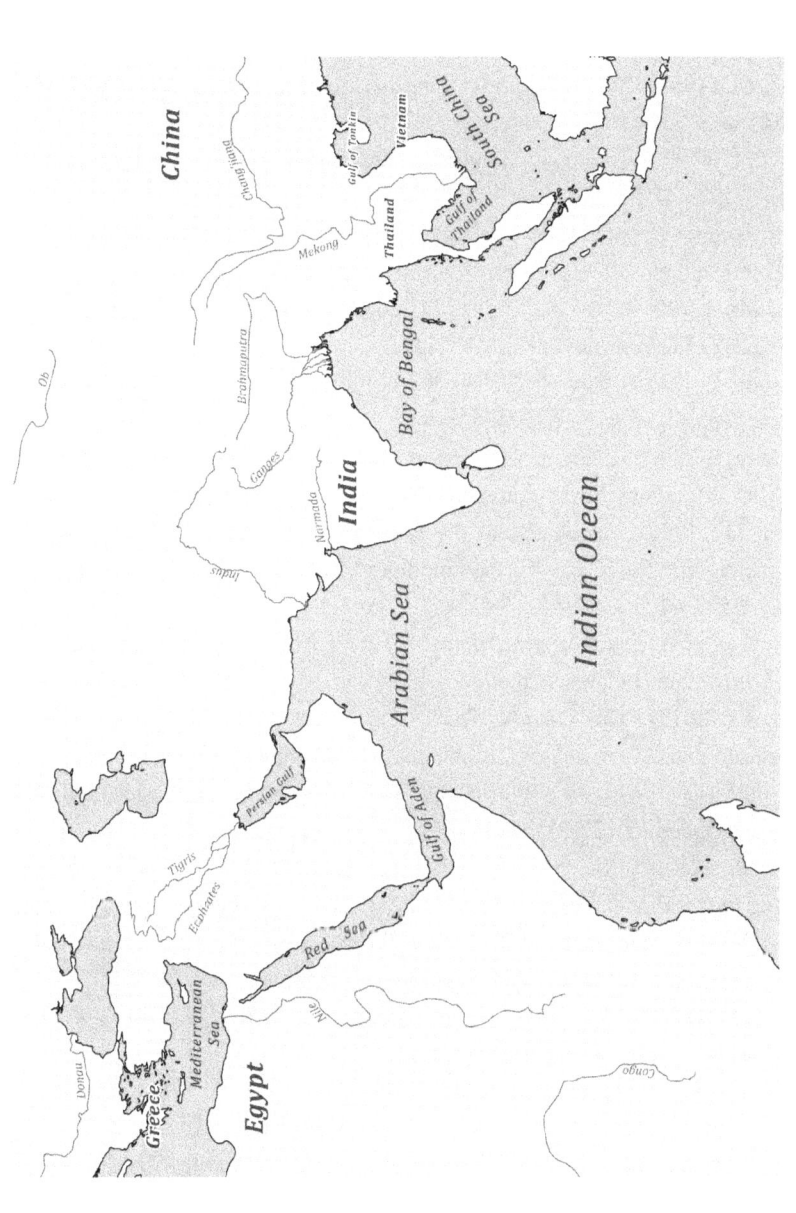

Figure A4 Map showing seas that connect Greece to Egypt, India, Thailand, Vietnam and China. Map drawn by Man Po Wong. This figure is also available in the online resources (www.cambridge.org/earlyglobalism).

References

Akira, I. 磯部彰. (1993). Saiyūki *keiseishi no kenkyū* 西遊記形成史の研究. Tokyo: Sobunsha.

Bakhtin, M. (1982). *The Dialogic Imagination*. Reprint. Austin: University of Texas Press.

Bantly, F. C. (1989). Buddhist Allegory in the *Journey to the West*. *Journal of Asian Studies* 48(3), 512–524.

Beal, S. (trans.) (1884). *Si-Yu-Ki: Buddhist Records of the Western World*. Reprint. London: Oriental Books Reprint Corporation.

Beauchamp, F. (2010). Asian Origins of Cinderella: The Zhuang Storyteller of Guangxi. *Oral Tradition* 25(2), 447–496.

Ben-Amos, D. (2010). Straparola: The Revolution That Was Not. *The Journal of American Folklore* 123(490), 426–446.

Bettelheim, B. (2010). *The Uses of Enchantment: The Meaning and Importance of Fairy Tales*. New York: Vintage Books.

Boucher, D. (1998). Gandhari and the Early Chinese Buddhist Translations Reconsidered: The Case of the Saddharmapundarika Sutra. *Journal of American Oriental Society* 118(4), 471–506.

Brown, R. (1996). *The Dvaravati Wheels of the Law and the Indianization of South-East Asia*. Leiden: Brill.

Casson, L. (2012). *The Periplus Maris Erythraei: Text with Introduction, Translation, and Commentary*. Princeton, NJ: Princeton University Press.

Cheah, P. (2008). What Is a World? On World Literature as World-Making Activity. *Daedalus* 137(3), 26–38.

Chen, J. R. 陳佳榮, Xie, F. 謝方, and Lu J. 陸峻嶺. (1986). *Gudai nanhai diming huishi* 古代南海地名匯釋. Beijing: Zhonghua shuju.

Cheung, M. P. Y., and W. Lin. (2006). *An Anthology of Chinese Discourse on Translation*, vol. 1. Manchester: St Jerome Publishing.

Chow, K. W. (2004). *Publishing, Culture, and Power in Early Modern China*. Stanford, CA: Stanford University Press.

Cunningham, E. (2011). *Zen Past and Present*. Ann Arbor, MI: Association for Asian Studies.

de Bary, T., and I. Bloom. (1999). *Sources of Chinese Tradition: From Earliest Times to 1600*. New York: Columbia University Press.

Deeg, M. (2008 [2010]). Creating Religious Terminology: A Comparative Approach to Early Chinese Translation. *Journal of International Association of Buddhist Studies* 31(1–2), 83–118.

References

Ding, N. (Ting, N.) 丁乃通. (1974). *The Cinderella Cycle in China and Indo-China*. Helsinki: Suomalainen Tiedeakatemia.

Ding, N. (1994). *Zhongxi xushi wenxue bijiao yanjiu* 中西敘事文學比較研究. Wuhan: Huazhong shifan daxue.

Dong, Z. 董志翹. (2002). *Guanshiyin yingyan ji sanzhong yizhu* 觀世音應驗記三種譯注. Nanjing: Jiangsu guji chubanshe.

Dudbridge, G. (1970). *The Hsi-yu chi: A Study of Antecedents to the Sixteenth-Century Chinese Novel*. Cambridge: Cambridge University Press.

Dundes, A. (1982). *Cinderella: A Casebook*. Madison: University of Wisconsin Press.

Fei, X. 費信. (1954). *Xingcha shenglan jiaozhu* 星槎勝覽校注, ed. C. Feng 馮承均. Beijing: Zhonghua shuju.

Goldman, S. J. S. (2021). *The Ramayana of Valmiki: The Completed English Translation*. Princeton, NJ: Princeton University Press.

Gómez, L. O. (1977). The Bodhisattva as Wonder-Worker. In L. Lancaster, ed., *Prajñāpāramit and Related Systems: Studies in Honor of Edward Conze*. Berkeley, CA: Institute of Buddhist Studies, 221–261.

Gong, Z. 鞏珍. (2000). *Xiyang fanguo zhi* 西洋番國志, ed. D. Xiang 向達. Beijing: Zhonghua shuju.

Guangxi Zhuangzu Zizhiqu gongyi meishu yanjiu suo 廣西壯族自治區工藝美術研究所. (1976). *Xiongdi minzu xingxiang fushi ziliao* 兄弟民族形象服飾資料. Guangzhou: Guangdong sheng gongyi meishu baozhuang gongsi.

Hansen, V. (2012). *The Silk Road: A New History*. Oxford: Oxford University Press.

Hansen, V. (2020). *The Year 1000: When Explorers Connected the World – and Globalization Began*. New York: Scribner.

Hao, C. (2020). *Dunhuang Manuscripts: An Introduction to Texts from the Silk Road*, trans. S. F. Teiser. Diamond Bar, CA: Portico.

Heng, G. (2003). *Empire of Magic: Medieval Romance and the Politics of Cultural Fantasy*. New York: Columbia University Press.

Heng, G. (2021). *The Global Middle Ages: An Introduction*. Cambridge: Cambridge University Press.

Hurvitz, L. (1976). *Scripture of the Lotus Blossom of the Fine Dharma*. New York: Columbia University Press.

Jameson, R. D. (1982). Cinderella in China. In A. Dundes, ed., *Cinderella: A Casebook*. Madison: University of Wisconsin Press, 71–97.

Lopez, D. (2016). *The Lotus Sutra: A Biography*. Princeton, NJ: Princeton University Press.

Ji, X. 季羨林. (1947). Futu yu fo 浮屠與佛. *Zhongyin wenhua guanxi shi lunwen ji* 中印文化關係史論文集. Beijing: Sanlian shudian, 323–336.

Ji, X. 季羨林. (1990). Zaitan futu yu fo 再談浮屠與佛. *Lishi yanjiu* 歷史研究 2, 2–11.

Ji, X. 季羨林. (1991). *Bijiao wenxue yu minjian wenxue* 比較文學與民間文學. Beijing: Beijing University Press.

Kao, K. (1989). Bao and Baoying: Narrative Causality and External Motivations in Chinese Fiction. *Chinese Literature: Essays, Articles, Reviews (CLEAR)* 11, 115–138.

Kasetsiri, C. (1976). *The Rise of Ayudhya: A History of Siam in the Fourteenth and Fifteenth Centuries*. Kuala Lumpur: Oxford University Press.

Levi-Strauss, C. (1973). Structuralism and Ecology. *Social Science Information* 12(1), 7–23.

Li, L. 李翎. (2008). Yi Guizimu tuxiang de liubian kan fojiao de dongchuan 以鬼子母圖像的流變看佛教的東傳, *Meishushi yanjiu* 美術史研究 4, 87–91.

Li, R. (trans.) (1995a). *The Great Tang Dynasty Record of the Western Regions*. Numata Center for Buddhist Translation and Research. Berkeley: University of California Press.

Li, R. (trans.) (1995b). *A Biography of the Tripitaka Master of the Great Ci'en Monastery of the Great Tang Dynasty*. Numata Center for Buddhist Translation and Research. Berkeley: University of California Press.

Li, S. 李時人, and J. Cai 蔡鏡浩, eds. (1997). *Dang Tang Sanzang qujing shihua jiaozhu* 唐三藏取經詩話校注. Beijing: Zhonghua shuju.

Liu, X. 劉昫. (1975). *Jiu Tangshu* 舊唐書. Beijing: Zhonghua shuju.

Luo, M. 羅懋登. (1984). *Sanbao taijian xiyangji tongsu yanyi* 三寶太監西洋記通俗演義. Shanghai: Shanghai guji chubanshe.

Ma, H. (1970). *Ying-Yai Sheng-Lan: "The Overall Survey of the Ocean's Shores,"* trans J. V. G. Mills. Cambridge: Cambridge University Press.

Mair, V. H. (1981). Lay Students and the Making of Written Vernacular Narrative: An Inventory of Tun-huang Manuscripts. *Chinoperl Papers* 10(10), 5–96.

Mair, V. H. (1983). *Tun-huang Popular Narratives*. Cambridge: Cambridge University Press.

Mair, V. H. (1986). Records of Transformation Tableaux (*pien-hsiang*). *T'oung Pao*, Second Series, 72(1/3), 3–43.

Mair, V. H. (1988). *Painting and Performance: Chinese Picture Recitation and Its Indian Genesis*. Honolulu: University of Hawaii Press.

Mair, V. H. (1989a). Suen Wu-kung=Hanumat? The Progress of a Scholarly Debate. In *Proceedings of the Second International Conference on Sinology*. Taipei: Academia Sinica, 659–752.

Mair, V. H. (1989b). *T'ang Transformation Texts: A Study of the Buddhist Contribution to the Rise of Vernacular Fiction and Drama in China*.

Cambridge, MA: Council on East Asian Studies Harvard University and Harvard University Press.

Mair, V. H. (ed.) (1994a). Buddhism and the Rise of Written Vernacular in East Asia: The Making of National Languages. *Journal of Asian Studies* 53(3), 707–750.

Mair, V. H. (ed.) (1994b). *The Columbia Anthology of Traditional Chinese Literature*. New York: Columbia University Press.

Mair, V. H. (2002). The *Heart Sutra* and *The Journey to the West*. In G. Wang, R. de Crespigny, and I. de Rachewiltz, eds., *Sino-Asiatica: Papers Dedicated to Professor Liu Ts'un-yan on the Occasion of His Eighty-fifth Birthday*. Canberra: Faculty of Asian Studies, The Australian National University, 120–149.

Mair, V. H. (2005). The First Recorded Cinderella Story. In V. H. Mair, N. Steinhardt, and P. Goldin, eds., *Hawaii Reader in Traditional Chinese Culture*. Honolulu: University of Hawaii Press, 364–367.

Mair, V. H. (2010). What Is *Geyi*, After All? In Alan K. L. Chan and Yuet-Keung Lo, eds., *Philosophy and Religion in Early Medieval China*. Albany: State University of New York Press, 227–264.

Mair, V. H. (2012). What Is *Geyi*, After All? *China Report* 48(1–2), 29–59.

Meyer-Fong, T. (2007). The Printed World: Books, Publishing Culture, and Society in Late Imperial China. *Journal of Asian Studies* 66(3), 787–817.

Milward, J. A. (2013). *The Silk Road: A Very Short Introduction*. Oxford: Oxford University Press.

Mu'an, S. 睦庵善卿. (1154). *Zuting shiyuan* 祖庭事苑 (*The Lexicon of the Ancestral Garden*). Kyoto: Nakamura Chōbei.

Murray, J. K. (1981–1982). Representations of Hariti, the Mother of Demons, and the Theme of "Raising the Alms-Bowl" in Chinese Paintings. *Artibus Asiae* 43(4), 253–284.

Nattier, J. (1990). Church Language and Vernacular Language in Central Asian Buddhism. *Numen* 37(2), 195–219.

Nattier, J. (1992). The Heart Sūtra: A Chinese Apocryphal Text? *Journal of the International Association of Buddhist Studies* 15(2), 153–223.

Nattier, J. (2008 [2010]). Who Produced the Damingdujing? 大明度經 (T225)? A Reassessment of the Evidence. *Journal of the International Association of Buddhist Studies* 31(1–2), 295–337.

Nattier, J. (2013). Now You Hear it, Now You Don't: The Phrase "Thus Have I Heard" in Early Chinese Buddhist Translations. In T. Sen, ed., *Buddhism across Asia: Networks of Material, Intellectual and Cultural Exchange*. Singapore: Institute for Southeast Asian Studies, University of Singapore, 39–64.

Nong X. 農學冠. (1998). Lun Luoyue wenhua yunyu de hui guniang gushi 論駱越文化孕育的灰姑娘故事. *Guangxi minzu yanjiu* 廣西民族研究 (4), 38–44.

Ouyang, X. 歐陽修. (1975). *Xin Tangshu* 新唐書. Shanghai: Zhonghua shuju.

Philibert, J. S. (1991). *Atom Movements: Diffusion and Mass Transport in Solids*, trans. S. J. Rothman. Les Ulis: Editions de Physique.

Ptak, R. (1992). The Northern Trade Route to the Spice Islands: South China Sea–Sulu Zone–North Moluccas (14th to Early 16th Century). *Archipel* 43(1), 27–56.

Ralston, W. R. S. (1982). Cinderella. In A. Duvandes, ed., *Cinderella: A Casebook*. Madison: University of Wisconsin Press, 30–56.

Red Pine. (2004). *The Heart Sutra: The Womb of Buddhas*. Berkeley, CA: Shoemaker and Hoard.

Rooth, A. B. (1951). *The Cinderella Cycle*. Lund: Lund University Press.

Roy, P. C. (1884–1894). *The Mahabharata of Krishna-Dwaipayana Vyasa*. Calcutta: Bharata Press.

Satapatha Brahmana. (1882). *Part 1: Sacred Books of the East*, vol. 12, trans. J. Eggeling. https://sacred-texts.com/hin/sbr/sbe12/index.htm.

Schmid, N. (2001). Tun-huang Literature. In V. H. Mair, ed., *The Columbia History of Chinese Literature*. New York: Columbia University Press, 964–988.

Sen, T. (2006). The Formation of Chinese Networks to Southern Asia, 1200–1450. *Journal of the Economic and Social History of the Orient* 49(4), 421–453.

Sen, T. (2015). The Spread of Buddhism. In B. Z. Kedar and M. Wiesner-Hanks, eds., *Cambridge World History, Vol. 5: Expanding Webs of Exchange and Conflict, 500 CE–1500 CE*. Cambridge: Cambridge University Press, 447–479.

Sen, T. (2017). Early China and the Indian Ocean Networks. In P. de Souza and P. Arnaud eds., *The Sea in History: The Ancient World*. Woodbridge: Boydell & Brewer, 536–547.

Sen, T. and V. H. Mair (trans. and annot.) (2005). The Tale of Master Yuan of Mount Lu. In V. H. Mair, N. Steinhardt, and P. Goldin, eds., *Hawaii Reader in Traditional Chinese Culture*. Honolulu: University of Hawaii Press, 304–339.

Sha, W. 沙武田. (2021). *Dunhuang bihua gushi yu lishi chuanshuo* 敦煌壁畫故事與歷史傳說. Lanzhou: Gansu renmin chubanshe.

Smith, W. (1867). Rhodopis. In *The Dictionary of Greek and Roman Biography and Mythology*, vol. 1. Boston, MA: Little, Brown and Company, 268.

Srisuchat, M. (2005). Mahabharata in Art and Literature in Thailand. *Indian Literature* 49(1), 105–14.

Strong, J. S. (1992). *The Legend and Cult of Upagupta*. Princeton, NJ: Princeton University Press.

Sun, H. (2018). *Transforming Monkey: Adaptation and Representation of a Chinese Epic*. Seattle: University of Washington Press.

Sutherland, H. (2011). A Sino-Indonesian Commodity Chain: The Trade in Tortoiseshell in the Late Seventeenth Centuries. In Eric Tagliacozzo and Wen-Chin Chang, eds. *Chinese Circulations: Capital, Commodities, and Networks in Southeast Asia*. Durham, NC: Duke University Press, 172–199.

Suwen 素聞. (2007). *Fahua jing daodu* 法華經導讀. Beijing: Zhongguo shudian.

Tagliacozzo, E. (2022). *In Asian Waters: Oceanic Worlds from Yemen to Yokohama*. Princeton, NJ: Princeton University Press.

Tan, Q. 覃清華. (2023). Huang Qing zhigong tu zhong Guangxi Zhuangzu fushi yishu tezheng jiqi chengyin 《皇清職貢圖》中廣西壯族服飾藝術特徵及其成因. *Wuhan fangzhi daxue xuebao* 武漢紡織大學學報 (6), 10–16.

Wade, G. (2004). The Zheng He Voyages: A Reassessment. *Asia Research Institute: Working Paper Series* no. 31, 1–27.

Wade, G. (2014). Beyond the Southern Borders: Southeast Asia in Chinese Texts to the Ninth Century. In J. Guy, ed., *Lost Kingdoms: Hindu-Buddhist Sculptures of Early Southeast Asia*. New York: Metropolitan Museum of Art, 25–31.

Waley, A. (1960). *Ballads and Stories from Tun-huang*. London: George Allen and Unwin.

Walker, H. S. (1998). Indigenous or Foreign? A Look at the Origins of the Monkey Hero Sun Wukong. *Sino-Platonic Papers* (81), 1–110.

Wan, M. 萬明. (2005). Ming Neifu chaoben "Feng Tianmin Sanbao taijian xia xiyang" zaju tanxi 明內府鈔本《奉天命三寶太監下西洋》雜劇探析. *Zheng He yanjiu* 鄭和研究 (1), 30–36.

Wang, L. 王麗敏. (2011). Datang Sanzang qujing shihua de zongjiao guannian ji zuozhe qianyi 《大唐三藏取經詩話》的宗教觀念及作者淺議. *Ming Qing xiaoshuo yanjiu* 明清小說研究 (99), 215–226.

Wang, Q. 王青. (2006). "Hui guniang" gushi de zhuanshu di: jianlun Zhong Ou minjian gushi liutong de haishang tongdao "灰姑娘"故事的轉輸地:兼論中歐民間故事流播中的海上通道. *Minzu wenxue yanjiu* 民族文學研究 (1), 13–18.

Wang, Y. (2021). *Writing Pirates: Vernacular Fiction and Oceans in Late Ming China*. Ann Arbor: University of Michigan Press.

Wang, Y. (2024). Mencian Reincarnation: Mercy and Forgiveness in the Seventeenth Century Chinese Novel *Predestined Marriage to Awaken the World*. *Journal of Chinese Literature and Culture* 11(2), 292–316.

Wei, W. 魏文斌 and Zhang L. 張利明 (2019). *Xiyouji bihua yu Xuanzang qujing tuxiang* 西遊記壁畫與玄奘取經圖像. Jiangsu: Jiangsu fenghuang meishu chubanshe.

Wei, Z. 維衹難. (2016). *Faju jing* 法句經. In *Dazheng xinxiu dazang jing* 大正新脩大藏經. *Chinese Buddhist Electronic Text Association*. https://cbetaonline.dila.edu.tw/zh/T2901.

Wivell, C. J. (trans.) (1994). The Story of How the Monk Tripitaka of the Great Country of Tang Brought Back the Sutras. In V. Mair, ed., *The Columbia Anthology of Traditional Chinese Literature*. New York: Columbia University Press, 1181–1207.

Wong, D. (2002). The Making of a Saint: Images of Xuanzang in East Asia. *Early Medieval China* 8, 43–81.

Wong, D. (2007). Guanyin Images in Medieval China, 5th–10th century. In W. Magee and Y. Huang, eds., *Bodhisattva Avalokitesvara (Guanyin) and Modern Society: Proceedings of the Fifth Chung-Hwa International Conference on Buddhism*. Taipei: Fagu wenhua, 255–302.

Wright, A. F. (1959). *Buddhism in Chinese History*. Stanford, CA: Stanford University Press.

Xu, Y. 許雲樵. ed. (1962). *Xia Xiyang zaju* 下西洋雜劇. Singapore: Shijie shuju youxian gongsi.

Yan, C. 嚴從簡. (1993). *Shuyu zhouzi lu* 殊域周咨錄. Beijing: Zhonghua shuju.

Yu, A. (ed. and trans.) (2012). *The Journey to the West*. Chicago: University of Chicago Press, 4 vols.

Yu, C. (2001). *Kuan-yin: The Chinese Transformation of Avalokitesvara*. New York: Columbia University Press.

Zan, N. 赞宁. (1987). *Song Gaoseng zhuan* 宋高僧传. Beijing: Zhonghua shuju.

Zhang, T. 張廷玉. (1974). *Mingshi* 明史. Beijing: Zhonghua shuju.

Zhao Q. 趙綺美. (1958). Longji shan yeyuan tingjing 龍濟山野猿聽經. In *Maiwang guan chaojiao ben gujin zaju* 脈望館鈔校本古今雜劇, vol. 5, *Guben xiqu congkan siji* 古本戲曲叢刊四集. Shanghai: Shangwu yinshuguan.

Zhou, Y. 周運中. (2018). Cong Wu Yexian gushi kan Tangdai Guangxi he Nanyang de Jiaowang 從吳葉限故事看唐代廣西和南洋的交往. *Yuanshi ji minzu yu bianjiang yanjiu jikan* 元史及民族與邊疆研究集刊(第三十五輯) 35(1), 180–188.

Zhu, Q. 朱慶之. (1992). *Fodian yu zhonggu hanyu cihui yanjiu* 佛典與中古漢語詞彙研究. Taipei: Wenjin chubanshe.

Zhu, Q. (ed.) (2009). *Fojiao hanyu yanjiu* 佛教漢語研究. Beijing: Shangwu yinshu guan.

Zhu, Q. (2010). On Some Basic Features of Buddhist Chinese. *Journal of the International Association of Buddhist Studies* 31(1–2), 485–504.

Zipes, J. (2000). *The Great Fairy Tale Tradition: From Straparola and Basile to the Brothers Grimm: A Norton Critical Edition*. New York: W. W. Norton & Company.

Zurcher, E. (1990). Han Buddhism and the Western Region. In W. L. Idema and E. Zurcher, eds., *Thought and Law in Qin and Han China: Studies Dedicated to Anthony Hulsewé on the Occasion of His Eightieth Birthday*. Leiden: Brill, 158–82.

Zurcher, E. (1997). *The Buddhist Conquest of China: The Spread and Adaptation of Buddhism in Early medieval China*. Leiden: Brill.

Acknowledgements

The SSRC transregional research short-term residency grant at the University of Southern California supported the completion of an early draft of this Element. The Faculty Research Grant from Lingnan University (grant number: FRG 101906) has fully supported the research and editing of this Element. Part of the HSSPFS from RGC of Hong Kong (grant number: 33000224) made it possible for this Element to be published open access, making the digital version freely available for anyone to read and reuse under a Creative Commons license.

Cambridge Elements

The Global Middle Ages

Geraldine Heng
University of Texas at Austin

Geraldine Heng is Perceval Professor of English and Comparative Literature at the University of Texas, Austin. She is the author of *The Invention of Race in the European Middle Ages* (2018) and *England and the Jews: How Religion and Violence Created the First Racial State in the West* (2018), both published by Cambridge University Press, as well as *Empire of Magic: Medieval Romance and the Politics of Cultural Fantasy* (2003, Columbia). She is the editor of *Teaching the Global Middle Ages* (2022, MLA), coedits the University of Pennsylvania Press series, RaceB4Race: Critical Studies of the Premodern, and is working on a new book, Early Globalisms: The Interconnected World, 500–1500 CE. Originally from Singapore, Heng is a Fellow of the Medieval Academy of America, a member of the Medievalists of Color, and Founder and Co-director, with Susan Noakes, of the Global Middle Ages Project: www.globalmiddleages.org.

Susan J. Noakes
University of Minnesota–Twin Cities

Susan J. Noakes is Professor of French and Italian at the University of Minnesota–Twin Cities, where she also serves as Chair of the Department of French and Italian. For her many publications in French, Italian, and comparative literature, the university in 2009 named her Inaugural Chair in Arts, Design, and Humanities. Her most recent publication is an analysis of Salim Bachi's *L'Exil d'Ovide*, exploring a contemporary writer's reflection on his exile to Europe by comparing it to Ovid's exile to the Black Sea; it appears in *Salim Bachi*, edited by Agnes Schaffhauser, published in Paris by Harmattan in 2020.

Lynn Ramey
Vanderbilt University

Lynn Ramey is Professor of French and Cinema and Media Arts at Vanderbilt University and Chair of the Department of French and Italian. She is the author of *Jean Bodel: An Introduction* (2024, University Press of Florida), *Black Legacies: Race and the European Middle Ages* (2014, University Press of Florida), and *Christian, Saracen and Genre in Medieval French Literature* (2001, Routledge). She is currently working on recreations of medieval language, literature, and culture in video games for which she was awarded an NEH digital humanities advancement grant in 2022.

About the Series

Elements in the Global Middle Ages is a series of concise studies that introduce researchers and instructors to an uncentered, interconnected world, c. 500–1500 CE. Individual Elements focus on the globe's geographic zones, its natural and built environments, its cultures, societies, arts, technologies, peoples, ecosystems, and lifeworlds.

Cambridge Elements

The Global Middle Ages

Elements in the Series

Late Tang China and the World, 750–907 CE
Shao-yun Yang

Medieval Textiles across Eurasia, c. 300–1400
Patricia Blessing, Elizabeth Dospěl Williams and Eiren L. Shea

The Chertsey Tiles, the Crusades, and Global Textile Motifs
Amanda Luyster

Swahili Worlds in Globalism
Chapurukha M. Kusimba

"Ethiopia" and the World, 330–1500 CE
Yonatan Binyam and Verena Krebs

Global Ships: Seafaring, Shipwrecks, and Boatbuilding in the Global Middle Ages
Amanda Respess

Elephants and Ivory in China and Spain
John Beusterien and Stephen West

The Global Legend of Prester John
Christopher E. Taylor

Islamicate Environments: Water, Land, Plants, and Society
D. Fairchild Ruggles

Teaching Early Global Literatures and Cultures
Geraldine Heng

Death Rituals: The Rūs and "Vikings" in Arabic and Persian
Tonicha M. Upham

Early Globalism and Chinese Literature
Yuanfei Wang and Victor H. Mair

A full series listing is available at: www.cambridge.org/EGMA

For EU product safety concerns, contact us at Calle de José Abascal, 56–1°, 28003 Madrid, Spain or eugpsr@cambridge.org.

www.ingramcontent.com/pod-product-compliance
Lightning Source LLC
LaVergne TN
LVHW011849060526
838200LV00054B/4244